D1612550

EAST COAST PASSAGE

EAST COAST PASSAGE

The Voyage of a Thames Sailing Barge

D. H. Clarke

Illustrated by Graham Humphreys

Longman

LONGMAN GROUP LIMITED
LONDON

Associated companies, branches and
representatives throughout the world

© D. H. Clarke 1971

First published 1971

ISBN 0 582 10374 6

To Kes—with thanks

*Printed in Great Britain by
The Camelot Press Ltd.
London and Southampton*

CONTENTS

LIST OF ILLUSTRATIONS

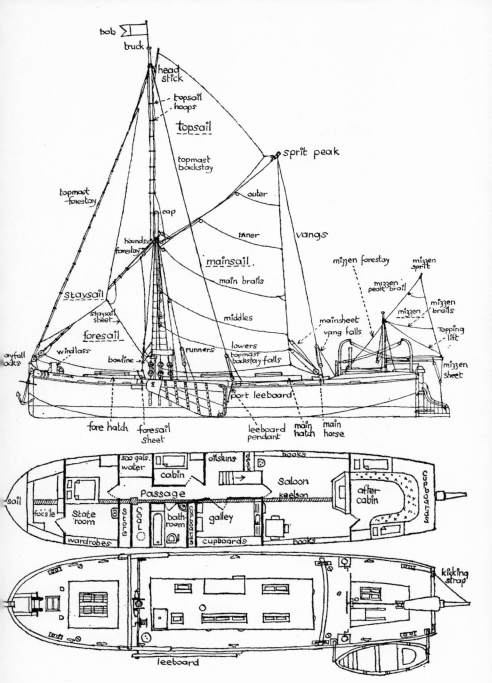

bob

truck

head
stick

topsail
hoops

topsail

sprit peak

topmast
backstay

topmast
forestay

outer

cap

inner

vangs

hounds

mizzen forestay

mizzen
sprit

forestay

mainsail

mizzen
peak brail

mizzen
brails

staysail

main brails

mizzen

mizzen
sheet

staysail
sheet

middles

mainsheet
vang falls

topping
lift

foresail

lowers

runners

mayfall
locks

windlass

bowline

topmast
backstay falls

port leeboard

mizzen
sheet

fore hatch

foresail
sheet

leeboard
pendant

main
hatch

main
horse

500 gals
water

oilskins

desk

books

cabin

Saloon

sail

Passage

keelson

after
cabin

foc's'le

State
room

store

coal

bathroom

cupboards

galley

wardrobes

cupboards

books

kicking
strap

leeboard

Sail, accommodation and deck plan

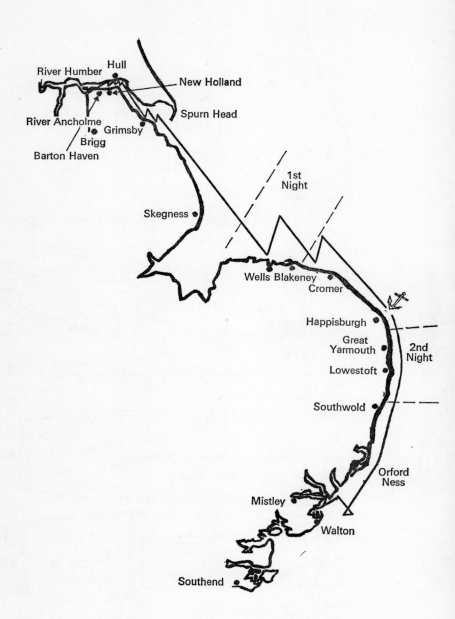

Overall route from Brigg to Mistley

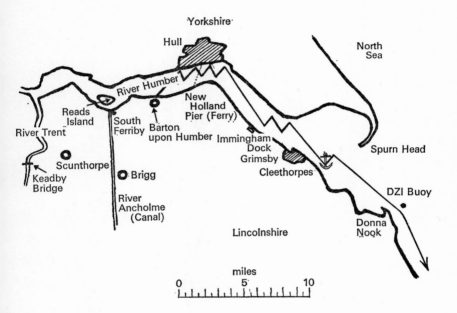

The worrying section: Brigg to Donna Nook

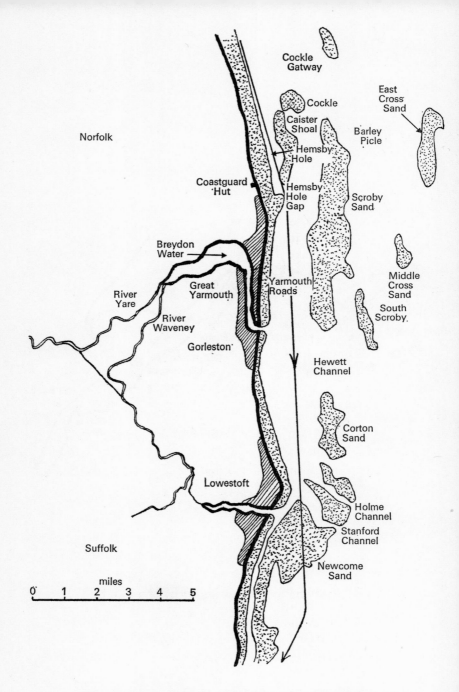

The nightmare section: Happisburgh to Southwold

1. GO YOU MUST

I awoke on that fateful March morning with a nasty sicky feeling in my throat: a recognisable symptom of incipient fear which will make a schoolboy attempt to fake an illness when he knows he is in for trouble at school that day. But I was nearly thirty-eight, war-proven, and I knew that what I had to do must be done; the sickness would pass.

I lay quietly in bed—Mollie was still asleep—and looked through the five-foot-square skylight, which covered the centre half of the forehatch, at *J & M*'s naked mast, topmast and spreet. Our bed was against the forward bulkhead, so that I was facing aft, and for the five years we had been moored in the same position by the bank on the canalised River Ancholme at the little market town of Brigg in Lincolnshire I had woken to the same view of those sturdy spars. Sometimes they had been wet and gleaming with rain, with the 54-foot spreet showering a cataract of water off its heel on to the deck just above the foot of our bed; sometimes they had been iced-up (that wonderland of a winter's morning awakening), and I would lie, warm and cosy, and think of the perils which men had faced under sail in Arctic and Antarctic waters; sometimes they would grunt and strain at their shackles as a gale swept across the flats of the Ancholme valley, and these would be good mornings to snuggle down into the womb of sheets and blankets and be thankful that we were not at sea fighting, as one must always fight the moment the protection of enfolding harbour walls are left behind. 'Grouse you may; go you must,' they used to say in the old square-riggers, and how right they were! Once a voyage has started the battle is on, and it is fought relentlessly to the death by wind, sea and all other natural forces. So 'go you must'—there is no let-up, no truce, no amnesty, until the arms of another haven gather you and your ship into safety.

But this fateful March morning was sunny. The 13-inch thick, 37-foot varnished pitchpine mainmast absorbed the rays and reflected warmth. The 12-inch thick black-enamelled spreet, and the 42-foot slender black topmast, both reflected an icy edge of light but otherwise ignored the sun. The scarlet ends of the peak and heel of the spreet and the scarlet 6-foot pole of the topmast, glowed like tips of cigarettes, and above all these, more than 70 feet over my head, the golden truck stood proud against the blue sky, although the frame of the bob squeaked a warning that there were some indications of a wind up there.

For nearly 22,000 days, *J & M*'s spars had greeted the dawn. Launched on 6 February 1897, by Mary Horsford at Sitting-bourne in Kent, 'This fine new topsail barge, *John & Mary*, was built at Mr Alfred White's yard' (the local newspaper had said); Arthur, Alf's son, told me fifty years later that she had cost £900: 'A bit expensive, but she was specially built for a skipper who had been with John Horsford & Company of Faversham for years.' He told me, too, that she was the only barge he knew which had always been known by her initials, although he didn't know why she had achieved this distinction. She had proved to be fast: 'Father copied her lines exactly when he built his best racer, *Sara*. He cut *J & M*'s half-model in the middle and whittled in a small piece; *Sara* came out at 87 feet against *J & M*'s 81 feet, but they both were the same otherwise, except they rockered *Sara*'s bottom by putting her on blocks fore and aft only. It was supposed to increase the speed, but I have my doubts. They were up to all sorts of tricks like that for the barge races, though a lot depended on the character of a barge.'

Mollie and I had heard a lot about the characters of barges in the immediate post-war period, when we decided that we would live afloat rather than spend our hard-won wartime

savings on a house which cost at least five times its pre-war
figure. The initial peace was very pleasant, but I foresaw that
it would not last; a new rat-race was about to start,
and I for one wanted out. Peace afloat seemed to me
more desirable than peace ashore. But there were still
problems.

'Most of father's barges had good characters,' Arthur had
rambled on, and there had been a wistful look in his eyes—
a longing, perhaps, for the lost past when he had been an
apprenticed barge builder. 'Always make enquiries about a
barge's character before you buy; it's much more important
than the price.'

We had taken this advice seriously, but there were other
facets to barge buying which included our own characters as
well as that of the barge we were seeking.

Does one ever know one's own character? And is a man ever
sure of his wife's character? I doubt it. If these things were
simple, then why the necessity of psychiatrists, marriage guidance bureaux or divorce? Oh, Mollie and I had known each
other in pre-war days when, without a care in the world, we
had sailed from a Westcliff beach out into the Thames Estuary.
Not together, of course; my period as a girl-hater lasted well
beyond adolescence, conned, no doubt, by a desire to be active
and to 'do things'. The facts that I started to sail when I was
twelve, and to fly when I was fifteen, undoubtedly were
instrumental in filling the otherwise empty gap suffered by
most teenagers who never know what to do with themselves
and inevitably are reduced to the much publicised sport of
sex—drugs and 'a cause' being more modern innovations.
Thus, although Mollie and I had known each other, we pursued
our separate ways until the accelerated emotions caused by war
enabled both of us to understand that we were, in fact, in love.
We were married in 1942, and separated (because war both
gives and takes) until 1945, when I was demobbed. For the
record, I came out after eight years' service with a couple of
gongs, a mention in despatches, and a retired rank of Squadron
Leader; retired, of course, because I retired from the Air

Force—they didn't retire me! A moot point, but one has to be firm when dealing with officialdom.

In case it should be thought that I joined the RAF for adventure, I must be strictly truthful and say that I didn't. The fact is that those voyages across the Thames Estuary whetted my appetite for more adventurous undertakings, and reading such classics as Robinson's *Deep Water and Shoal*, Stock's *Cruise of the Dream Ship*, and Slocum's *Sailing Alone Around the World*, and many others, convinced me that *this* was true adventure. Because I knew how to fly, and because I loved flying, I applied to join the RAF with a four-year Short Service Commission, concluding (at the time, accurately) that my pay (commencing at 11s 10d per day), plus my gratuity after leaving (£300), would be sufficient for me to purchase my dream ship and to sustain me during a protracted solo circumnavigation.

I saved enough money to pay £150 for *Axelle* in 1939. She was a straight-stem gaff cutter, built by George Wickland of Tenby in 1910; 36′ 0″ × 32′ 0″ × 10′ 6″ × 5′ 6″, teak on oak, with a 10-foot bowsprit, an ancient Kelvin sleeve-valve engine, and bird's-eye maple panelling in the 6′ 6″ headroom saloon. I paid cash, flogged the engine for £25 (I was a sail purist in those days), and still had a bank account in the black—which was pretty good saving really, because I have always liked my beer and I wouldn't give that up for anything.

Mollie, to some extent, shared my enthusiasm for sailing. Coming as she did from a mercantile marine background (her grandfather had sailed in such famous clippers as *Patriarch* and *Thermopylae*; her brother is a Master Mariner), I took rather too much for granted and assumed that she would enjoy life afloat. She had joined the WRNS early in 1940, and consequently was the proud owner of a very low service number, but, like me, she did not take kindly to service discipline. That she remained in the WRNS until VE day, when she could have walked out at any time without repercussions (a unique, and little-known situation which applied only to the WRNS during World War II), is indicative of Mollie's character:

she had volunteered, so she stayed. In a similar fashion, she volunteered for a life afloat, and although this time it was not the discipline which upset her, I failed to grasp the simple principles which govern the nesting habits of all females. The rule is that they must have a secure nest during the breeding season—and I am afraid that a wandering sailing vessel does not come into this category.

After a search lasting nearly a year, which included inspecting the bodies and souls of more than fifty Thames Barges, and conversing with a much greater number of people in order to ascertain the character of each craft, we bought *J & M* for £525. She was still trading in grain when I bought her, and I reasoned that she must be in fair condition to survive the war and still be capable of carrying a dry cargo.

For the war had almost wiped out the remnants of the Thames Barge fleet which had been declining steadily since the beginning of the century. The heyday of these amazingly efficient sailing machines had been in the latter half of the nineteenth century, when there had been at least 4,000 trading on the London River—some historians say as many as 8,000! But at the change of the century, the numbers had declined to just over 2,000, and by the end of World War II to just over 300; in 1950 there were 102 left, and in 1957 23; three years later, only 7 were left, and in 1970 the sole surviving trader was the mule-rigged spritsail coasting barge *Cambria*, owned and skippered by Bob Roberts. Now, in 1971, there are none.

So be it. In 1947 I prognosticated this decline, declaring in an article that trading barges would disappear completely by about 1957. I was a bit out, but the fact remains that they died, quietly, to await an inevitable revival when the public decides to rediscover the beauty, the power, the mechanical perfection of the Thames sailing barge—just as they have done with veteran cars and aeroplanes, antiques, and practically anything which was created with skill, perfection and, yes, *feeling*. The Plastic Age cannot compete with these things.

Yet to stand on the deck of a barge, and gaze aloft at this most complicated rig of all sailing ships, is not conducive to thinking beautiful thoughts. For example, you have to be a much better than average car owner before you can drive a veteran, and certainly you have to evolve a new philosophy in order to look after the mechanical needs of such an acquisition. But a veteran car can only break down—and at speeds which, almost certainly, will not cause harm to anybody. After buying *J & M*, the awful truth dawned on me that although I knew how to sail, I didn't know how to sail *this*— neither did I have the vaguest idea of how I would look after her!

To some extent I was also a little worried about her character. 'Happen she'll suit,' I was told by an Essex man, who had worked her as mate in the Starvation 'Thirties. 'Tetchy ould bo't that'll fare; *do*, that'll think o' suthen head masterous similar-same any mawther. Yis. Yis. I doubt you'll like her ways, maister.' He had said many other things, most of them incomprehensible, but I gathered the general trend. *J & M* was inclined to get herself into tight corners, but she was very skilled at getting herself out of them—like any woman. I liked that touch; in due course we discovered that she did indeed get herself into the most impossible scrapes, but 'similar-same any mawther', she always managed to survive.

I am no woman's man—never have been—and perhaps this was why, right from the beginning, I was always nervous of *J & M*. She overawed me. Often I would find a sheltered corner on her broad decks, and try to merge myself into her, but I never entirely succeeded. (I'm a great one for finding sheltered corners in the sun, so helpful for quiet orderly thinking, brooding or navel-contemplating. I have the greatest admiration for philosophers in the days of yore—solitary, sunny, sheltered corner-seekers all, I feel quite sure.) This was a new experience for me, because ten years before I had merged easily and naturally into every aircraft I had flown and every car or motor-bike I had driven; and although I had not had the chance to sail *Axelle*, I had merged with her too. But with *J & M*. . . .

In the first year of ownership, I stripped every bit of gear out of her—or, at least, a boatyard in Kent did most of it for me. Then, over a period of two years, I laboriously put everything back. As far as I was concerned the accommodation was relatively unimportant (this was all done professionally, and completed by 1950), but the hull, the spars, the sails, the lee-boards, the rudder, the anchor, chain and windlass, the mast-case, the winches, the standing and running rigging—the *working* part of her—was very important. I cared for every-thing; nothing was skimped.

Fortunately, this was a period when it was easy to replace worn-out fittings, at little or no cost, with gear from other barges. From 1945, Kent and Essex creeks and backwaters were choked with barges which had given their final service to man during the war as traders, floating warehouses, ammuni-tion ships, mine-spotters, rescue ships (Dunkirk in particular), and many other duties. Now they were unkempt, worm-ridden, rotting, and, above all, uneconomic misfits.

So the forgotten barges gave *J & M* those items which they would never again use themselves. *June of Rochester* gave the lower portions of her oaken windlass bitts to make a well-seasoned taffrail; *Utility* gave setting booms, a hitcher, a new mizzen spreet, and two mast-case dollies; *Band of Hope* and *Dabchick* gave a mast-case dolly each; and *Mid-Kent* gave an almost new mast-case; a fleet of a couple of dozen London and Rochester Trading Company barges, all with masts lowered, mildewed sails rotting on the decks, rain-sodden holds lumbered with tangled rigging, and hulls which groaned and trembled as they wrung to the shape of the uneven mud under their flat bottoms, gave wire and blocks and shackles and rope and deadeyes and chain. And sundry hulks, star-scattered in the almost unexplored wastes of other Kent and Essex creeks all had some treasure to offer—until eventually *J & M* wore a little something of the last possessions from about thirty barges. It was as well that they were there, for I had little to offer except time and muscle—and solitary thoughts about my responsibilities towards my barge, my wife, my son and my life.

Kester was six months old when we moved aboard, and I was in no doubt whatsoever how he had complicated the growing list of my responsibilities. I wanted to opt out of the rat-race, but already I had found that whilst the philosophy of escapism is sound enough, the practice is well-nigh impossible.

I had, of course, neglected to clarify to myself from what I was escaping—all I wanted was out; many a person with much greater educational talents than I has made this error. Although I recognised my responsibilities, I failed utterly to see that I was creating a small self-contained world which inevitably would

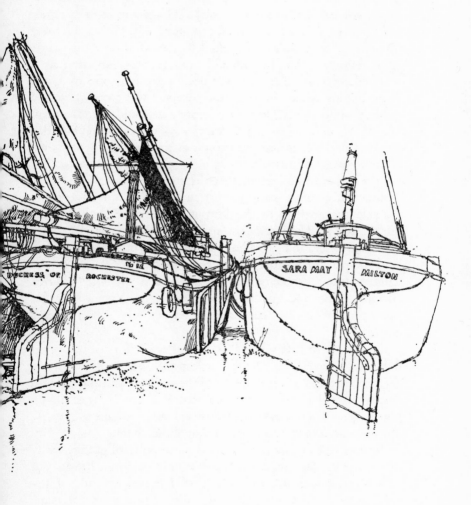

turn into its own rat-race for survival. There is no escape—anywhere. At best you can change your environment, or you can die. Death is the only sure escape from living.

Figures were, and still are, all that matter: figures which represent money, which in turn represents respectability. My total savings once *Axelle* was sold amounted to £1,700; by the time *J & M* was fitted out and ready for sea, in 1948, my capital was entirely invested in her. It was at this stage, after eighteen months unpaid, unrelenting labour that I realised the truth. I have never been a grouser, but, by God! now I knew what 'go you must' meant. I was committed to a pattern of life which, suddenly, I foresaw would never be easy; the worth of security, which Victorian-lingerings had installed in my mind, clamoured in protest at the commitment which I had imposed on myself.

Yet I was quite certain that the insecurity was more than compensated by a pattern of living which moved entirely outside the artifices of the known world. If you have read H. G. Wells' *The Invisible Man* you will know what I mean. Mollie, Kester, and I lived a different life in our creek in Kent, and the passing horrors of that period—coal shortages, power cuts, housing problems, rising prices, and the like—swirled around the area, but never affected our haven. For by that time we were very nearly an entirely self-contained unit.

I must admit that when *J & M* was ready for sea I thought I had achieved my goal of freedom. However, as soon as I straightened my aching back from the labours of fitting her out, and surveyed my financial position, I realised that although until then I had eschewed such mundane problems as money, now I would have to do something about them.

It would seem that my acquired philosophy of getting away from it all was based on the flimsiest of foundations, but actually this was not, and is not, so. The primary rule of any adventure is: first establish your base; if you wish to escape from a rut, then it is essential that you have somewhere to escape to. This rather elementary and obvious fact is so often missed by so many! Well, my base was now established and it was up to me to evolve a system whereby we could survive financially with a minimum participation in the rat-race. That, to this day, I am still striving to solve this particular problem, is indicative of its complications.

The squeaking of the bob slowly refocused my eyes from the blue of the past to the problems of the present. Mollie had not stirred, and I had been back-tracking for—I looked at the clock—just ten minutes. What wonders can be performed in the computer we call a brain! As the relays snapped out, the automatics took over: I slid out of bed, dressed, cooked breakfast for Kes and myself (Mollie had never been a breakfast-lover), and performed those daily functions which are so essential for the rest of the day to run smoothly. This is the only rut I allow: the personal habits of living. And, of course, whilst the automatics take over, the conscious mind can think . . . and plan.

Eleven years had passed since I bought *J & M*, nine since we had first set sail in our floating base. Nine years of adventure in a thousand guises. And now, for the umpteenth time, an era had finished, and our mutual decision was to head south to home waters. *J & M* had to be re-rigged and completely fitted out for the passage; I had no job, no prospects, and just over £150 in the world. But I had a good breakfast in my stomach, and the sicky fear had gone. I lit my first pipe of the day on deck, and watched the rat-racer's cars pouring across New Bridge towards Scunthorpe.

Yesterday was the end of the old adventure; today was the commencement of a new exploration into the unknown. I crossed the gangplank to the grassy river bank to begin my preparations.

2. INITIAL PROBLEMS

To captain a sailing vessel which can load 115 tons of cargo, without being born into the trade, is difficult enough; to act as ship's husband to such a craft, on a bank balance which teeters on a razor's edge (although personal pride had never allowed it actually to fall the wrong way), is a nagging worry, equivalent to survival problems in a desert when one has neither food nor water to start with; but to labour single-handed on a barge, preparing her for sea—*this* is the greatest problem!

The giant curtain of *J & M*'s mainsail must have weighed over a ton; it was as much as I could do to lift even the tiny mizzen—probably it slightly exceeded a hundredweight with brails and shackles fitted—awkwardly shaped as it was, even when folded flat. The mizzen, and the undressed staysail (66 feet on the hoist, 10 feet across the gore) were the only sails which could be flattened; the others were 'made up', folding luff to leech, or tack to luff, over and over, until thickness and weight prevented further bending. Tied with a dozen or so individual two-inch rope 'stops', the fore-, top-, and main-sails resembled three elongated red slugs, which could just be carried on the shoulders of seven, nine and eighteen men respectively. But I only had me—and Kester. As a final resort I had Mollie.

It is still said—albeit without much thought—that a sprit-sail barge could be handled by a man and a boy. As a matter of fact, during the nineteenth century many a barge was sailed by a man and his wife! But the 'boy', or the 'wife', were not exactly of the same stock as ourselves: mostly they were born to a life of toil and struggle in a physical sense;

ours was more of a mental upbringing than acceptance of grinding labour as a way of life.

Not that we were a weak team in either sense. I am a six-footer, weighing around thirteen stone, and Mollie tipped five foot eight and ten stone, then as now. But Kester was only ten, rising eleven, and lacked the weight so necessary for handling the heavy gear, although what there was of him was all bone and muscle, thanks to his life afloat; he was sculling a barge skiff when he was five, and that exercise alone is sufficient to build up a very taut body. Physically we were as fit as we could ever be.

Mentally, as a husband and wife team, we were disturbed, but determined. For most of her stay *J & M* had lain in the same berth, facing north towards the Humber, some one hundred and fifty yards south of the New Bridge, on the east bank of the river. She was the biggest ship ever to arrive at Brigg, and in the early days she had created considerable interest. Now, she was an accepted colourful landmark— and landmarks are not expected to move. But ships are creatures of the sea, and when they are deprived of the sluicing joys of their natural element they desiccate and die. *J & M* had so suffered. Her port side had faced west—and most of each day's sun—for too long; her starboard side had been attacked by the dampness from the river bank or by icy, drying, easterly winds. Her three-inch-thick pitchpine decks had taken the brunt of all weathers without a drop of sea-water to relieve their agony: salt water retains moisture and pickles wood; fresh water, in which she had floated for five long years, only wets to rot—an insidious decay. I had tried to prevent her from drying-out, but my puny efforts with deck bucket and river water had been no more helpful than they would have been to a stranded whale. *J & M* had dried out— that was the major disturbing truth.

The problem would have been simplified if barges had been built as conventional craft with seams which can be caulked. But they were not. Two layers of $1\frac{1}{2}''$ pitchpine planking, with a mixture of tar and elk or cow hair between them (sometimes cow dung), and rabbeted seams, were difficult to refurbish. You should never caulk a rabbeted seam, which is rather like half a tongue-and-groove, because you are liable to split the 'tongue' half at the back. But some of those seams gaped so much I could stick my fingers into them, and that was desperate all right! Only careful and constant maintenance had prevented rot; she was sound for her age, but very leakworthy.

Desiccated: that exactly describes the condition of our vessel when I started to fit her out. All her resilience had gone. It was as if every part of her had been dustily entombed under a pyramid for a thousand years—every part, that is, except her underwater surfaces, and that area of greatest danger, her waterline. Here the interplay 'tween wind and water can promulgate rot quicker than anywhere else if it is neglected, but I had made sure at every tarring that she was listed well over before I scraped and finally applied the brush. Yes, even in spite of Mollie's grumbles from the galley, when a list to port for one day, followed by a list to starboard for another day, ruined comfortable cooking. *J & M* didn't leak a drop in her Brigg berth, but in a seaway . . .

All ships must 'work': that is to say, every part of them must have some allowable movement. Build a rigid ship (if it were possible), and it would grind itself apart at the first sign of bad weather. A barge, of necessity, is a *very* flexible vessel. She must be capable of sailing light, with nothing in her hold, of loading part of a cargo forward or aft, or taking a concentrated weight amidships; she must be prepared to dry out on any ill-shaped berth (and sometimes she will scream in protest!), with or without a cargo, and she must 'pick-up' without leaking; she must face a storm at sea, loaded, when the seas will invade the decks and strive to batter in the hatches. So she must be able to 'hog' and 'wring', without making water, and because she is a flat-bottomed vessel and has no curves to relieve the strain, she has to rely on her keelson as her major fore and aft support.

Once, all barge keelsons were wood: fourteen inches square or larger, this backbone extended from stem to transom, dividing the sealing (floor) of the hold in half with its bulk. But as the supply of such great timbers declined at the turn of the century, steel keelsons took their place: girders, bolted channels, inverted 'tee' sections. *J & M* had a 15" × 6" girder, with wood-padded sides to prevent grabs from hitching the keelson out of her when unloading.

The keelson alone cannot support the length of a barge. Flexibility is so essential, and the hogging strains in a flat-bottomed craft are so great, that every fore and aft member must assist in the work. It was for this reason that a quality barge always avoided butts in deck and hull planking—and, indeed, sometimes wales and chines. A gap in a length of plank was a weakness and a potential source of leaks. So the pine sealing, oak inner and outer wales and inner and outer chines, and the pine lining between them, the double-skin rabbeted planking, the stout decks—even the oaken hatch sides —should preferably all have been in one length. Unfortunately, in *J & M*, repairs and replacements over the years had broken into the pattern and there were many butt-joints; it was impossible to decide whether she had ever been otherwise. And like a railway line in cold weather, the gaps at the butt-joints had widened to an alarming degree.

Then there were her weaknesses—and the secret of these I had always kept to myself, for I had never wanted to worry Mollie over and above the general awe which she suffered whenever we had sailed our floating home. There were many weaknesses—and many soft spots too. The bulk of her size, and the size of her construction, gave confidence of massive strength, but the strongest part of a chain is the weakest link, and *J & M* had quite a list.

There was, for example, the slightly loose lower gudgeon which held the bottom pintle of the massive rudder hinged to the stern-post. That had been weakened in 1947, when I had missed the notorious Wallet Spitway, which splits the Gunfleet at the northern entrance to the London river, en route to Brightlingsea, and run *J & M* aground near the South-West Gunfleet Buoy in a sou'westerly gale; anchored, and half dried-out, she had pounded her stern as the bows rose to every breaker. She had survived that night of danger, but she still carried this scar.

Then there was her port leeboard. In spite of examining every derelict barge in our travels (which almost always were stripped of their leeboards), and searching every abandoned barge-yard, I had never been able to find a good replacement. The starboard one was in excellent condition, but the port 'wing' had wet-rotted along the seams, which now gaped and exposed the part-rusted through-bolts. Although the lee-boards were eighteen feet by six feet, each weighing about a

ton, in rough seas I could only be happy on the port tack—
there was always a chance that the port leeboard would give
way to the fantastic strains when we were on the starboard
tack.

J & M's leeboard winches were of the unconventional
vertical capstan type—not the more usual horizontal wind-
lasses, or 'crabs'. Even working barges were notorious for
slack-teethed winches, but the capstan type is dependent on a
snug-fitting vertical shaft to ensure smooth turning of the
pinion, and *J & M*'s were badly worn. There 'was a knack
in cranking them—and you had to have weight behind you; I
was the only member of the crew with both assets.

Another unconventional *J & M* variation was her davits,
which were fitted to port instead of the more usual starboard
position. The forward davit, through-bolted to the covering-
board, tended to be a trifle rickety because part of the wood
under the rail had rotted. Not much—but enough for me to
worry about.

None of these points were *major* worries—I would not have
gone to sea if they had been—but a conglomeration of niggling
minor snags can soon mount up in one's mind to an over-
whelming fear that the whole issue will crumble into decay
at the slightest sign of trouble. By keeping these worries to
myself, and not sharing them with Mollie, I suffered to this
extent.

There was some rot in the stem apron—once again not
much, but it had meant in the past that I had had to refasten
the planking into the stem on the starboard side whenever it
had sprung slightly. Then again, the round of the starboard
bow, some ten feet from the stem, had quite a bit of rot in the
inner skin. I had discovered this ten years before when I
had removed the lining in the fo'c's'le during the accommoda-
tion-building days; would she leak here when she began to
shoulder heavy seas?

I had checked, by means of a taut string, the hog of the
keelson and discovered that it was humped nearly six inches
amidships. This meant that her long immobility in fresh water

had not done her much good, since the unsupported 'ends' had sagged quite a bit. I knew that barges would hog after a time, even in a flat mud-berth—they usually straighten with the next cargo—but had *J & M* become too lazy, or too senile to straighten her creaking spine? A rockered hog is fair enough, since it undoubtedly improves the tacking qualities and is supposed to increase the speed, but I worried in case the reversed hog of my barge was enough to prevent her from going about at all.

To set oneself a dangerous task, verging on the impossible, is always mentally exhausting. In spite of considerable previous experience in personal adventure, I found that this time I could not counter worrying thoughts with pleasurable activity because very nearly everything was my responsibility but I was no longer responsible just for myself. This tended to act as a brake to my otherwise natural exuberance and overwhelming optimism. So even before I started work, I was appalled at the hopelessness of the venture.

There was *J & M*, sixty years old, carefully maintained, but only as a houseboat, with two tons or so of sails and running rigging stowed ashore some distance from her berth—unchecked for five years. There were her naked masts and spars, weighing something like three tons, which had to be checked and rigged.

There were all the myriads of faults about her vast hull, which I knew as intimately as the shaving area on my face—some of them, seemingly, impossible to restore to a seaworthy condition. And all this had to be achieved on a capital of £150, singlehanded, with wife and son responsibilities (Kester must not be away from school any longer than was absolutely necessary)—oh yes! and dog and cat responsibilities too: our nine-month-old Alsatian, Sym, and our two-year-old cat, Tigger.

Most depressing of all was our inability to decide where we should go. South from the Humber, means up to London to sailormen, or up to the London river. But we wanted neither. We wanted another berth, at least as comfortable as our Brigg mooring, and not too far from a suitable job for me; neither of these requirements could be found in London, and probably not on the London river. Even if they could, I would not have gone: I had abandoned London in 1937, forsaking for ever a predestined career in my father's printing business; nothing would induce me to return to that soul-destroying rut area again.

So from a bright start of adventurous intent, it did not take me very long to descend into an abyss of hopelessness, without the mental energy to get the job started. It was ridiculous to try! Why, even skilled sailormen disliked the treacherous east coast passage—and all they had ever had to do was sail from A to B or from B to A. I hadn't even started to consider the worries of the actual voyage, and yet the task already seemed impossible.

I did consider going south by train and looking for a job, and then a nearby berth; I dismissed this as impractical through lack of money. I did reconsider staying in Brigg and re-searching for another job—but I had already tried this and I knew that the Suez crisis had caused considerable unemployment in Scunthorpe and surrounding areas. I did think of trying to sell *J & M* as she lay; as a matter of fact she had been up for sale for a year already, but there had been no enquiries: money was tight, and who would want to buy a sixty-year-old engineless barge? The pros and cons churned monotonously in my head, increasing the worry without finding a new solution. There was really only one answer: head south.

When faced with a difficult, and therefore dangerous task, I am not one of those keen bash-on-regardless types who so often (and annoyingly) not only survive all the vicissitudes, but invariably achieve a lucky break in the way of publicity or some other form of monetary gain. My reaction is always to sit back and question the feasibility of the project. Is it possible, I ask myself, that this job can be tackled in a totally different manner? Often it can, but this form of hang-on-a-minute-I-want-to-think is not as image-promoting as the more easily recognisable do-or-die type of adventuring. I can only uphold my methods with the self-evidence that I survived the war, which for me included three volunteer suicide jobs and the usual variations in squadron defence and attack; having flown at Dunkirk, in the Battle of Britain, on the first fighter sweeps over France, and with the advance from Alamein to Tunis, with three trips on a catapult-armed merchant ship in the Battle of the Atlantic and several other side-issues of varying importance. I recognise my inadequacies, but at the same time I know that I cannot alter my tactics.

So when, after a good breakfast and a determination to start work, I subsided into miserable introversion, I was not surprised. I had suffered in this way so often that I had come to accept the misery as an initial part of any adventure in which I indulged. The monotonous rotation of ideas continued to whirl in my head, getting me nowhere: all were negative, and I could find little or no satisfaction from enforced optimistic thinking.

Basically, I tried to convince myself, *J & M* is a sound barge: hadn't she made the passage north, in 1952, against continuous strong nor'westerly winds, including a gale, in eight days? Why, even barge skippers had said it was impossible. Of course, Mollie and Kester had stayed behind on that occasion and I had only three inexperienced men as crew, but three *men* represented more muscle-power than one woman and a child. (A depressing thought.) *J & M*'s gear had stood up well to that pounding: off Skegness, a half-hour squall which had crept up to 48 m.p.h. (confirmed later by anemometer records at nearby North Coates Fitties aerodrome) had very nearly dismasted her; closehauled on the port tack, bows driven under so that the whole of the starboard deck had been a maelstrom of churning water, with her port chine well clear of the racing seas, she had staggered on and survived without damage. The strains of that voyage had certainly caused her to leak badly; presumably she would leak just as badly again. (More depression.) The back-breaking deck pumps had not been able to cope with the leaks, and the four of us had fought a losing battle at this soul-destroying, muscle-jerking grind; only by

getting her into sheltered waters did we finally win. (Mollie
and I wouldn't have a chance if she leaked as badly again.)

And there I was, back to the depressing thoughts about the
hopelessness of the situation.

Condition reports and fitting-out worries, plus the complications of prognosticating the future, were but a part of the whole
process which delayed the start of the venture. A tight community such as ours must, and does, develop its own rut of
living, and this, too, had to be considered. My hesitancy to get
cracking was caused primarily by my knowledge of the enor-
mity of the task, but the undercurrent of disruption of the
ordered routine was undoubtedly a contributory brake.
We all sensed it—especially Sym and Tigger—and none wanted
that slow crumble into chaos which inevitably follows a
period of contentment.

We had no need to discuss this aspect between ourselves.
Our long living and loving together had evolved a partnership
which did not need chatter to let each of us know what the
others were thinking of doing. In the early days, neither
Mollie nor I appreciated this unique situation. She, in her
natural function as mother, prepared her nest, and suckled
her young to the best of her ability; I, in the manner of all
males, found the food and defended my property against all
potential enemies: man and nature. Both jobs were entirely
time-consuming. Such are the rules of civilisation, unfortunately, that direct access to food is difficult—in towns, impossible;
also, the requirements of our ship could not always be met by
robbing the hulks of the dead. Thus, money was a necessity,
even if the earning of it was time-consuming.

From an already full life, therefore, hours had to be found
grudgingly for this purpose, which lessened the time available
in every day when I could attend to our ship and my family.
So, when I was absent, protecting *J & M* became an additional
chore for Mollie, and in due course for Kester.

To speak of a wife as a 'chief mate' or a child as 'crew' is
ridiculous; a woman's work afloat, unless she captains her own
ship or is a professional, will never allow her to be more than

a temporary stand-in as a very un-able seaman; to demand all of a shore-based wife's multitudinous services to her husband whilst at sea reveals an inefficient and unimaginative skipper. We eliminated this absurdity by sticking to our natural functions as far as possible; I no more wanted to nurse the baby than Mollie wanted to sail our ship. As the years passed, we each became expert in our own jobs, and, when under duress, amateurs in each other's jobs.

Kester assimilated knowledge from both of us. There was much for him to learn. Whilst electricity and mains water were installed in most houses throughout the country, Kester learned the intricacies of paraffin lighting and butane heating, hose-connections and header tanks. The vagaries of nature, too, had to be understood thoroughly because of the troubles which they brought: prolonged sunshine meant future deck leaks, rain always produced those leaks, prolonged rain might encourage rot, frost and snow meant frozen water or butane pipes—and future deck leaks, wind meant chafe aloft and alow, gales meant possible danger to moorings, and so on. Every variation of weather carried a different threat to our combined comfort, and nearly always necessitated some action or reaction. Sewage disposal was about the only function aboard which was as simple and as foolproof as in a house—although the complications of a marine lavatory called for considerably more than house-plumbing knowledge if Kester happened to drop a marble into the basin (which he did on more than one occasion), and the supply of flushing water was infinitely more involved than just pulling a chain.

From the hardships of part-conversion, to the comfort of a fully-converted accommodation, did not ease the chores. To port, amidships, Mollie now had a well-fitted galley, 12′ × 8′, with Rayburn cooker (for hot water and oven cooking), and Calor stove (for quick boiling and grilling), and more than adequate cupboards, shelves and working surfaces. There was an 8′ × 8′ bathroom, with a 6′ 6″ bath, a wash-basin, a Downton W.C., and a walk-in airing cupboard. The saloon was 22′ × 16′ and boasted a large brick fireplace disguised as an inglenook under the main-horse deck; the asbestos chimney from the Esse-Dura stove extended through the bulkhead into the after cabin and utilised the deck flange at the forward end of the den-head which had originally served the crew's cooking stove. The after cabin was unaltered —I had even retained the original golden-grained paintwork— except that I had fitted and plumbed a fold-up wash-basin to the forward bulkhead. The door to the after cabin passed under the companionway, the ladder of which was generally stowed in the fo'c's'le unless we were at sea. The floor here was some twelve inches higher than in the saloon—a point of some importance in a leaking ship, as will be seen. With our double cabin under the forehatch, the single cabin to starboard amidships, the fo'c's'le and the stowage space under the mast deck, there was 1,060 square feet of floor space in our floating home, which was comfortably adequate.

Cool in summer and always warm in winter, well-lit in daytime by the large skylights, and at night by a variety of paraffin lamps, we were very nearly as self-contained as can ever be possible in England. With full water tanks (800 gallons), paraffin tank (30 gallons), coal bunker (5 tons), Calor gas bottles (unlimited), refrigerator, ($4\frac{1}{2}$ cubic feet, paraffin operated), and the necessary food, we could remain independent of the shore for a month or more—depending on how much water we used. Reduced to yacht-cruising rations of one gallon per head per day for all purposes, we could have stayed at sea for forty weeks—ten months!

Self-contained—and self-sufficient: each to their own jobs, with Kester serving a unique apprenticeship, but all capable of wearing skirt or trousers without too much discomfort whenever the circumstances required a turnabout. In this way we were each taught how we were part of our ship, and so our partnership was complete. I cannot say that I enjoyed wearing a skirt any more than Mollie enjoyed wearing trousers, but since it was *J & M* which nearly always dictated the work which had to be done we soon learned that it was essential to get on with the job regardless of sex. It is of interest to note that Mollie had to wear trousers literally, for most of the time, as is the case whenever a husband and wife team go to sea in a boat; if the situation were reversed, literally, would yachting be such a popular sport?

So our partnership developed because there was no alternative. The demands of our ship were insatiable; we never caught up. When the initial joys of conversion faded we realised that we had created a monster which, unlike Frankenstein's humanoid, required constant and loving attention: constant, because her age had reduced her defences and she always needed assistance of some sort; loving, because she was our home, she was beautiful, and undoubtedly she had a likeable character. Furthermore, she was all my capital. If she had been a house, we could have locked her up, put her in the hands of estate agents, and sold her. We could not do this to our barge: to leave her for even a short period would have induced nature to attack in force—just dampness alone can cause havoc in an old vessel; to expect a quick sale of a large engineless sailing ship was a hopeless dream—on two or three occasions, when we had run into some additional worries, we had put her on the market: there had been no takers! And so we had had to go on, destined, like the crew of the *Flying Dutchman*, to tread her decks seemingly forever; worse, to tend to her needs for a lifetime. We were as much a part of our monster and she was a part of us, and we were parts of each other. We had discovered the true meaning of partnership.

This was not all. The blackmail which she imposed on us thrust the first thin sliver of a wedge between Mollie and myself. Womanlike, my wife sensed the pattern before I did, and began to hate her adversary. It may be trite to mention the eternal triangle, but the pattern began to form.

A great deal has been written about affection between man and inanimate objects—generally those which are antique. Seldom is any mention made of the faults of the inanimate party. The loving, then, is one-sided, with acute paranoia to combat against. 'I am magnificent; I am beautiful; I am unique; I am irreplaceable,' the Monster seems to say. 'It is your duty to expend all your money, all your energy, all your life, in looking after me. I am the greatest. I was created by a Master. Kneel, serfs, and slave to preserve me and the glories of the past which I represent.'

Fortunately for me, I recognised the symptoms of paranoia in *J & M* even before I sailed her to Brigg. I tried to sell her, without success, but I tried hard to refuse to yield entirely to her demands. 'You can bloody wait,' I would tell her, but woman-like she would press her claims for attention by making the point in question more obvious; generally she won because there was no alternative.

A marriage partnership which is becoming divided by the intrusion of an inanimate object is a rather ridiculous situation. To be unable to escape from the association is positively macabre. *J & M*'s spreet swung above our heads like the Sword of Damocles.

These thoughts we shared without need for discussion. It was no more necessary for *J & M* to inform us that she was too old to tackle the East Coast Passage, than it was for Mollie to say that the only hope of selling our Monster was to get her into home waters. It was no more necessary for me to tell *J & M* that although I was very fond of her I would never allow her to come between Mollie and me, than it was for me to offer explanations to Mollie. We knew that the voyage had to be made, and that the partnership could not be broken until we reached a safe haven somewhere in the south; in effect, I said to *J & M*: 'I have looked after you for eleven years, and now you must do your very best for us.' This is the sort of idiocy to which one is reduced when dealing with Monsters.

The Sword of Damocles hung, and the cogs of the Wheels of Destiny meshed, as had been decided by whatever laws govern these things. I had done my best to think of an alternative route; I had tried very hard to put a bold face to the venture: in neither case had I succeeded. We—*J & M*, Mollie, Kester, Sym, Tigger and I—would go because we had to go, together, as a partnership. . . .

That was the snag: there was no foreseeable future!

3. PRELIMINARY SKIRMISHES

Archimedes, or some such genius, was reputed to have declared that given a lever long enough he could move the world. Like most scientific-minded people, he avoided the basics: how would he get the lever into position before he could demonstrate his one-finger exercise? Once upon a time apprentices, whose trade required the use of tools, were taught how to make them without the use of tools so that they could fit themselves out with a set in order to become apprentices and learn the trade.

I had neither served an old-time apprenticeship, nor could I loftily proclaim from a pinnacle of theoretical science. However, I had been shipmates with my barge long enough for her to teach me a great deal; furthermore, as a result of the first two years of ownership which I spent fitting her out, I had taught myself that nothing, really, in the weight-lifting and shifting game is impossible. Had I not re-shipped her two-ton rudder whilst lying in a mud berth? Had I not lifted her heavy mast on board and stepped it singlehanded? Had I not launched her across fifty yards of slimy mud as a result of a bet?

(Oh, the time it took before I found the confidence to start!)

First, the sails and running gear.

Five years before, they had been stowed in the loft of a nearby garage belonging to . . . I think a very fair name for him would be Uncle Fred. (You don't find people like Uncle any more—he was once an apprentice who made his own tools, which started with digging up the iron ore and burning his own charcoal—and certainly you will never again find a garage like his, entirely self-contained, yes, even to having his own water supply and making his own electricity.) At the unrigging

I had received more than adequate help from interested on-lookers, who afterwards had displayed red-ochre-stained hands, necks and shoulders with some pride. But now there were no onlookers. Very well, I would have to use a lorry.

The obvious choice was our coalman, Hopalong—so-called because of one deformed leg which he dot-and-carried like a jolly peg-legged sailor just home from the sea. Hopalong owned his coal business and he was very proud of it. He had dreams of expanding—happy, cheerful dreams of a large thriving family business which could afford to pay its men excellent wages, and give its customers first-class service. As it was, good men were impossible to find, and for most of the time Hopalong had to do everything himself. Occasionally I had given him a hand, and he had been grateful. Now I wanted some help, and I knew that he wouldn't let me down. 'Sure, Nobby,' was his answer. 'Give me a hand with deliveries this afternoon so I can get finished early, and then we'll drive straight down to the garage and load up.'

This was how coal delivering became one of the eighty-odd different jobs which I have tackled in fifty years.

Hopalong duly backed his lorry into Uncle Fred's spacious barn, and it was easy enough to tumble the sails, wire, blocks and rope from the loft into the back. A short drive down to New Bridge, a careful reversing right up against the stile, and the unloading was just as easy. 'Thanks a lot,' and Hopalong was off to his tea—and just inside the stile a mountain of gear awaited removal.

It took me a whole day to move that mountain into the field on the other side of the sea-wall. First I carried the easy stuff—coils of wire and rope, and bundles of blocks. Next I dragged, end by end, the foresail; then the topsail. From my struggles with these lighter sails, I knew that I would never move the mainsail in this way, and I began to despair again as I worked out the laborious moves which I would have to make before I could get that ton of canvas and rope into the field with the rest of the gear.

Finding mechanical assistance on a barge is easy. The

anchor windlass has the most, and can move tons. The dolly
winch, mounted over the windlass, has no gearing apart from
the leverage supplied by the length of the handles, but the
drum carries a length of wire with a rope tail (*J & M* had
fifty fathoms of three-quarter inch flexible steel wire and five
fathoms of one and a half inch tarred Italian hemp), which is
almost as good as a third hand when it comes to pully-hauly
work. Then there is the main brail winch, the four mast
dollies (two direct and two geared), and the two leeboard
winches which are fitted with warping drums. Potential
lifting tackles are available everywhere—the runners, topmast
backstays, wangs,[1] etc.—but the main one on *J & M* was a
chain double-burton with a rope fall which was permanently
bent two-thirds up the spreet. Finding a source of power was
simple; organising the power was laborious to the extreme.

First I had to find out how much power I needed.

I ran out the dolly wire, through the block attached to the
forestay, direct to the mainsail. It was not long enough. I
broke out a suitable length of two-inch rope from the fo'c's'le
and attached this to the dolly tail, and to the large eye-splice
in the ten-inch circumference headrope of the mainsail which
fitted over the peak of the spreet and was its sole support. Then
I carried the one-hundredweight kedge anchor from its stowage
aft under the steering box to a position five points off the starboard bow just on the other side of the sea wall, and with a
spade dug it into the ground so that the fluke would not drag.
I broke out a snatch-block, shackled it to the anchor, and
fitted the dolly wire into the sheave. Then I tried to winch the
sail along the sea wall. After a dozen journeys between winch
and sail (each return trip grossing at least three hundred yards),
I managed to straighten the mountain into an elongated slug—
but the winch was not nearly powerful enough to drag the
weight of the sail along the ground.

[1] Spreet and wangs should be spelt sprit and vangs. However,
I think that it is easier to write what is said, rather than worry
about the correct spelling. Wangs are always wangs; spreet alters
only in the word sprits'l.

To shift the dolly wire on to the main windlass meant removing the bower anchor chain. I slipped the dogs, a two-fingered steel claw chained to the deck just forward of the windlass, over the anchor cable and gently let the chain out until the dogs held the full weight of the anchor. Then I passed the tail of a short length of rope, which was kept permanently bent to the stout iron bar which I had fitted between the tops of the windlass bitts, under the three turns of anchor chain around the barrel, and heaved these tight under the bar. The barrel was now free for use. Because of the strain on the forestay, I led the dolly wire through a stouter block which I shackled to the foresail tack eye-bolt on the stem head, and looped it around the windlass barrel so that it wound onto its tail. Then I fitted a handle and began to crank.

Instead of pounds, I was now applying tons, and I knew that something had to give: either the sail must move, or one of my fitments would not stand the strain. The kedge dragged! I slackened-off, dug a fresh hole, put a short plank across the fluke, and tried again. This time everything held. Slowly the slug crept along the sea wall until it was in a position opposite J & M. Of course, this necessitated moving the kedge into a second position astern of J & M, which meant digging another hole and realigning the dolly wire, but after six hours of continuous labour I moved the mountain to Mahomet, rolled it down the steep slope into the adjacent field, unfastened the stops and bit by bit spread it out, returned all equipment used into stores, re-rove the dolly wire, and tidied up.

Total time taken to fetch the sails and gear from Uncle Fred's dry loft into the field: fourteen hours, plus three hours coal-heaving. Two days had passed.

I had never discovered the true age of J & M's sails. When I bought her, opinion was expressed by a sailmaker that they were 'at least twenty-five years old'. That was eleven years before. Five years in a barn loft had aged them visually: pigeons, hens and other roosters had sprayed guano; sparrows, martins and sundry nesters had made their homes; rats and mice had lived, at least partially, off the health-giving red ochre and

fish oil dressing with which they were coated. Armed with
chalk, the next morning I walked my acreage of canvas and
marked for repairs. It was not a cheerful task. Then I checked
the standing rigging, listing necessary replacements. Even
more depressing. Then the running rigging, and I soon discovered that sisal did not survive five years' stowage: most of it
was brittle and needed renewing.

I put this bad news to the partnership that evening.

'We'll need three hundredweight of two-inch sisal and a
hundredweight of two and a half inch,' I told Mollie after
Kester had been put to bed; 'about thirty yards of Number
Three repairing flax, three cops of seaming twine, fourteen
pounds of spunyarn, ten fathoms of three-inch Indian hemp
(some of the lanyards need replacing). Then for dressing the
sails we'll need the usual hundredweight of red ochre and
half-hundredweight of yellow ochre, and ten gallons of fish oil.
The main brails need replacing, so we'll want a hundred and
twenty feet of one and a half inch wire—24 by 6 if I can get it.
And I'll have to get some charts; the last lot will be out of date
by now.'

'How much is all that going to cost?' she asked.

'About £30.'

The fire glowed comfortable warmth in the saloon. Mollie
knitted; the radio played. Some rain spattered on the decks and
coachroof. I cursed, and hurried ashore to roll up the sails
which were outspread in the black field. It took me twenty
minutes. The rain slowly increased to a steady downpour and
I was already too late to keep them dry, but I finished the
job in order to save myself the laborious process of getting rid
of puddles the next day. I should have remembered that it
always rains when barge sails are spread out on the ground!
As I dragged the rapidly stiffening canvas, luff to leech, tack to
luff—over and over—to remake three slugs, I groused, alone;
the cold rain ignored my blasphemies.

Once the machinery of fitting-out is started, it gathers
momentum. A phone call to a commercial chandler in Grimsby
produced all my requirements the next afternoon: more weight

to shift from the stile to the field! Now I had to find a fifty-gallon drum for mixing the sail dressing; a visit to Uncle Fred was successful, and Kester could fetch it after school. Then back to the sails which I had spread out before breakfast: they were dry but very board-like, thanks to the wet ground. I walked on them; they crackled. Conditions were far from being ideal. A cold, damp wind blew across the naked field. I fetched palm and needle, thumbed the first length of twine through the eye, and started off with herring-boning the simple slits and tears and chafes.

I must admit that when I started to learn sailmaking in 1948 I enjoyed it. My teacher was a young lad who had just completed his apprenticeship at a famous racing barge sail loft. I liked it so much that he and I reopened an old loft at Faversham in which, many years before, square sails had been made for coasting brigs and fore-and-aft sails for fishermen. As with churches, builders of sail lofts always picked an advantageous position, and once we had cleared a space in the loose hay (for it was now part of a farm), and opened the double-doors which overlooked the narrow creek, we could sit at our benches in the sun and contemplate the scenery which included the two miles of twisting creek down to the Swale. There I had learned palm and needle work on large sails and a little about the complexities of shaping new sails; there I had sat, very happily, whilst my right and left hands had learned to operate as automatically as any sewing machine—round seaming, flat seaming . . . hundreds of yards of each, with the triangular shaped needle pricking through dozens of bolts of No. 0, No. 1, No. 2 and No. 3 flax canvas, and sometimes through double-o or even treble-o. The click of the needle in the little metal cup of the palm, the grasping by three fingers of the thick flax and the contraction of the hand which drives the needle through, the finger and thumb grip and jerk follow-on which snatches the doubled twine through the canvas, with the left hand pulling the bight and snapping the stitch tight, became as automatic as the once-per-second slow beat of my heart. To seam, and contemplate, is not arduous labour.

But in an open field, with a North Sea moisture-laden breeze blowing, wet underfoot, and damp canvas to sew, the pleasure is dissipated and the grinding toil becomes painfully obvious. The already vast area of sail seems to spread outwards towards limitless horizons. 'Start with the biggest,' I thought, 'and you will have broken the back of the job.' A week later I was still working on the mainsail—and the topsail, foresail, staysail and mizzen threatened at least as much again.

Of course a professional might have been quicker, but not very much, I fancy: modern sailmakers are not accustomed to working in such conditions. As my right finger and thumb muscles reattuned to the labour, and the area on the top of the base of my thumb re-hardened to the drag and chafe from the sail-palm, the automatics took over as before. It was a painful process—re-establishing unused muscles always is— but in due course I was flat seaming at as good a rate as was possible in the circumstances. A week passed before I was ready to turn the mainsail, but by then I was over the hump of the physical grind and beginning to freewheel.

Apart from dampness and cold and weather problems, repairing large sails in a field involves sewing every stitch to grass. You cannot take a sailmaker's bench to a sail which weighs a ton; instead, you must crouch over the repair area like an Eskimo at his hole in the ice and ply your needle direct to the flat canvas. The method of pricking the needle through, lifting the canvas with the tip, using the fulcrum of the first finger, and driving the needle up and through, collects a blade or two of grass at every stitch. When the sail is turned to complete the flat seaming of any patches applied, the surface resembles an attempt to make a camouflaged haystack! 'Here's something you can do to help,' I told Kester, and I showed him the thumb-against-knife-blade method of removing the tufts; it took him hours.

The monotony of this sort of labour is its one saving grace. When muscles are attuned, and the hump is crossed, there is nothing left but to continue: day after day, week after week. The routine deadens thought; the mind no longer bothers to worry. To be frozen, cold, warm or hot made little difference to my pace. Only rain stopped play. I was very lucky, because after that initial night's downpour it only showered on two or three occasions.

And then, quite unexpectedly, I double-sewed the end of a seam, searched for the next chalk-mark, and discovered that I had finished. I stood up, felt the warmth of the sun, walked across to *J & M*, lifted the galley skylight and peered in. 'I've finished the sails,' I told Mollie. 'Good,' she replied; 'I was just going to call you. Lunch is ready.' 'How long have I been?' I asked. She looked at the calendar. 'Nineteen days—and this morning,' she said. Lunch smelled delicious; I had no recollection of eating nineteen previous lunches.

'How much money's left?' Mollie wanted to know when we had finished eating. I checked my accounts: 'Just over £76.'

'Can we do it?'

'Just about.'

'What have you got to do next?'

It seemed almost a pity that I had to re-submerge myself into worry again. Outside, *J & M*'s sails made a perfect picture of the sailmaker's art—well, perhaps not perfect from the professional sailmaker's point of view, but certainly as good as could be expected from the working conditions, the age of the sails, my limited skill, and the lack of money. What had seemed like screwed-up bundles of red hardboard were now, I knew, seamanlike engines of driving power. I was proud of my work.

'Dress the sails,' I told her, and I actually looked forward to doing it.

I found that Kester had delivered the fifty-gallon empty oil drum. Somebody—either he or Uncle Fred—had cold chiselled off the top, and cleaned the interior with Teepol. Must have been Uncle Fred who did the chiselling, and Kester the cleaning. . . .

Strictly speaking, the dressing should be made with seawater, although there has always been a difference of opinion about this. I had no alternative—river water it would have to be. I half-filled the drum by bucket. Now the messy part. Three-quarters of the red ochre, half the yellow ochre, stir well, add six gallons of fish oil, stir well. It was too late to start dressing, so the final adjustments to the water/oil/ochre content would have to wait until next morning when they could be balanced to suit the weather. I spent the rest of the daylight reeving a new lanyard through the deadeyes of the starboard middle shroud. The rest of the daylight? Listen . . .

Cut three fathoms from a coil of three-inch tarred Indian hemp. Make a double Matthew Walker at one end and whip the other. Cut away the old lanyard. Reeve the new lanyard so that the Matthew Walker lies snugly against the sole non-recessed hole in the upper deadeye, then down through the opposing hole in the lower deadeye. Unhook the forepart of the starboard runner and bend the tail of the new lanyard to the hook with a Blackwall hitch. In order to lengthen the scope of the runner tackle, unhook the after-span of the starboard runner, and re-hook it further aft—either to the topmast backstay chain plate, or to a short length of chain passed under the rail at a convenient scupper. Take the fall of the runner tackle to the lower starboard mast-winch. Wind taut. Belay. Seize the first and second lanyard reeving with spunyarn. Slack off. Reeve the lanyard through the centre hole of the upper deadeye and down through the centre hole of the lower deadeye. Blackwall hitch to runner; set up tackle as before; seize third and fourth reevings. Reeve the lanyard through the remaining top hole, down through the last bottom hole, set up tackle and seize fourth and fifth reevings. Finally, hitch the tail of the lanyard to the shroud, or, if there is sufficient length to spare, sheet-bend through the elongated wire splice which surrounds the upper deadeye. Finish by seizing the tail to its standing part. Total time for one person doing all his own fetching and carrying: two hours twenty minutes.

The next day, because I wanted sunshine for dressing the sails, it rained. The forecast had warned me, and the sails were all made up, and covered, to keep them as dry as possible. But the rain had ruined my simple pleasure of contemplating

the routine of the past three weeks and bringing it to a satisfactory conclusion. Nature is very clever at upsetting routines.
So I tackled the main brails in the fo'c's'le.

J & M's mainsail was controlled by five sets of brails which,
as has been so often noted, operate in exactly the same way as a
theatre curtain. There were the rope outer and inner brails
which controlled the peak and the upper part of the leech,
the rope middles and lowers which kept the foot of the mainsail
more or less together (these brails have always had a richly
deserved bad reputation for getting taffled!), and the wire
main brails upon which one relied entirely for shortening
sail. The power for the job was supplied by the main brail
winch bolted to the deck on the port side of the mast. *J & M*
had a good one—almost new. The wire was carried permanently
bent on the drum, and the winch was never normally used
for any other purpose. The cleats for the inners and outers
were on the after shrouds, on both sides; the middles and
lowers were cleated to both sides of the mast case.

It has been said that a Thames spritsail barge has the most
complicated rig of any sailing ship which has ever been
rigged. I never doubted it. It has also been said that this ingen-
ious rig was evolved bit by bit, until it reached perfection, and
that any further changes would reduce handling efficiency.
Well—maybe. I tried to improve on one or two items, but
never succeeded. Yet there *were* snags: the middles and lowers,
for example. And there were weaknesses.

Discounting breakages in the standing rigging, I thought
that the most dangerous were the main brails and the wangs.
If either parted, there was hardly anything the skipper could
do. It is true that he could get the mainsail under partial control
by taking the inner and middle brails to the mast winches, but
in strong winds the untamed belly of the sail would flog and
flog until something else parted. If a wang went whilst at
anchor in a seaway, control of the spreet would be lost, and
long before a temporary repair could be effected by using one
of the rolling wangs the appalling power of the sweeping
spreet would either break it in half or tear the mainmast out

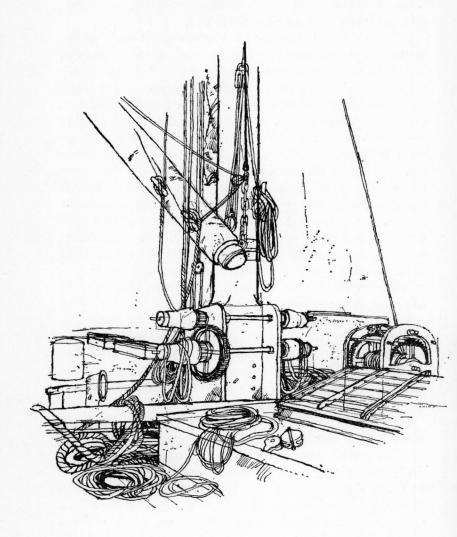

of her—for a barge at anchor has a terrible roll, as I had discovered on several occasions when we had rolled scuppers
under in strong wind-against-tide conditions.

So as a result of past wang and main brail experiences, and
subsequent worries, I had given her new two and a half inch
wire wangs and manila double tackles long before I sailed her
north; now the main brails were due for renewal (although
I had no doubt that they would have been considered adequate
by any old-time barge skipper).

In these days of mechanical swageing, the art of wire-splicing
is rapidly disappearing. I suppose there still are professional
riggers who can tuck a splice in wire, but I doubt if there are
very many who can operate without a vice. It is an art within
an art, for splicing wire is a hazardous undertaking even when
everything is in your favour. The worst I ever tackled in
J & M's fo'c's'le were the two and a half inch wangs; compared
with those four splices around thimbles, the two needed for
the main brails, plus one marrying splice to unite them to a
single tail, were easy—and the 24 × 6 composition of the wire
rope (six lays each of twenty-four strands, with a hemp core)
made the job almost a pleasure.

But the rain rattling on the curved Perspex hatch (which I
had made in the early days to give more light to this notoriously
dark area) reminded me that natural forces were awaiting, just
outside, for the setting forth: the final commitment to battle.
Pre-action nerves seldom relax enough to allow scope for
pleasure—unless alcohol is used. Overnight parties relieved
this strain during the war, but now I couldn't afford the luxury.

And we were, as yet, only halfway into battle.

4. THE LONELINESS OF COMMAND

Kester said, 'Nobby', and I surfaced slowly from contemplating a small section of sail which I was using to test my sail dressing. It was a perfect morning for the job: blue skies, sun warm, ground drying rapidly after yesterday's rain, birds singing. . . . Even the grey Ancholme, reflecting the mood, sparkled and danced. I had started the day by setting up another new lanyard, to give things a chance to warm up and dry out, and by mid-morning I was ready to start on the sails.

Surprisingly, the red-yellow ochre mix, so beloved by marine painters, is a delicate combination which must be carefully tested before applying. Too much water or too much ochre, and a shower of red dust will cover the decks within a very short space of time; too much fish oil, and the vast folds of the brailed sails will stick together—permanently, if they remain brailed for a time—and certainly they will crack and tear if too much oil is allowed to dry out completely. There must be just enough to lubricate the flax from chafe and bind the ochre to the fabric, with sufficient water to apply the ochre evenly; and the mix of the red and yellow colouring must be balanced as carefully as any painter grinds and blends his pigments and oils, because it would be an affront to any barge if the shade was too deep a red, or too yellowish. There were precedents; the colour *had* to be right.

So I had tested the basic dressing which I had mixed two days before by stirring it thoroughly and brushing a square foot of mainsail with the result. Give it a couple of minutes to soak in, I was thinking. . . .

'Nobby,' Kester repeated, for he was very used to my slow recovery from contemplation to conversation, 'can I help?'

48

I said 'yes' reluctantly, because an additional hand meant extra organisation. I had the sole soft-bristle broom on board, but there was another head in the fo'c's'le. When Kester volunteered for a job I never liked to put him off, but more often than not the work entailed in employing his labour merely added to my endless chores without achieving very much advantage. Now I had to remove the handle from the hard-bristle broom which Mollie used on board (preferably without her knowledge!), fit the soft-bristle head to it (which, as I had suspected, meant cutting one inch off the foot of the handle and reshaping it), and afterwards cleaning the handle thoroughly, reshaping it again, and refastening Mollie's hard-bristle head to it. Total time, probably twenty minutes or more—not much, but it meant further effort over and above the planned grind. I took Kester with me to show him what I had to do; next time (I hoped) he would be able to tackle the job himself.

The sun had dried the water of the dressing on my test patch by the time I got back, and I felt the surface and checked the oil content by rubbing what had come off between thumb and finger. The colour was too yellow, and there was insufficient oil. I added two shovelfuls of red ochre, a bucket of water and two gallons of oil, got Kester to stir thoroughly, painted another patch of sail, and tested again. The colour was right, but there was too much powder; more water needed. I repeated the test. Not quite enough oil. I added a gallon and tested. Just right. I repeated the test on the topsail. Again it was just about right. We could start work.

'Lunch up!' Mollie called from the deck, and I cursed silently. Although I had so often experienced the swift passing of time whenever I had plodded through any labour connected with my barge, I had never ceased to be amazed by it. Five hours had passed, and all I had achieved that morning was a new lanyard set up, one broom-handle fitted and the sail dressing mixed correctly.

As I brooded through lunch, checking and rechecking all that I had done and all that I would have to do, it occurred to me that although my time was my own it was still trickling away as wastefully as it did when I hired it to an employer. Was such a project as ours a waste of time—even when there was no practical alternative? Was I merely delaying an inevitable catastrophe by wasting my time on servicing my barge to the best of my ability? Far, far ahead I was aware of the folly of the voyage itself, and yet I knew that it was quite impossible for me to stop what I had started. The sails could not be left in the field now: they must be bent on to *J & M*'s massive spars. Once she was fitted-out, she and we had to go somewhere. There was only one practical direction we could sail—south. It seemed to me that there was little or no difference between our project and the struggles of any person between womb and grave: once the environment has been established, the involvement is decreed, and so the rules of that involvement must be learned even if it takes a lifetime. Go you must! The pattern is always the same. There is no escape. A cliché-ridden politician, steering his ship of state, must be as involved in his expedition as we were in ours.

The seconds, the minutes, the hours drift away into the past, and sometimes, very occasionally, a mark is recorded. Out of the billions of creatures who have lived and died since the world began, how many have achieved such a distinction? The percentage must be infinitesimal. And yet each and every one has battled through a lifetime to achieve something, just as we would have to do on this voyage. Like them, I could not possibly know where I would finish the voyage, or what would happen to us when we reached the final haven, yet I—we—wasted time with careful preparations in exactly the same way as a child, through teenage to adulthood, is rigged and fitted-out by parents in preparation for his or her voyage through life. In these circumstances I was fully aware that luck played a more important part than skill, although skill must predominate in order to survive at all. I have always maintained that the correct proportions should be around 65 per cent skill and 35 per cent luck for survival in adventure, action, or life itself. If this delicate balance alters, then the chances of survival decrease at an alarming pace: skill without luck being, perhaps, fractionally safer than luck without skill.

Kester was eager to get to work on the sails after lunch, and I showed him how the dressing must be brushed thoroughly into every nook and crevice. He started on the mizzen, and I worked on the mainsail; then he dressed the foresail whilst I did the topsail. The staysail on a barge is never ochred. By the end of the afternoon we had completed one side of the sails.

Once dressed, I knew that it would be dangerous to make them up. The oil-water mix can soon build up a tremendous heat in a confined space, and I had actually seen what had happened to a mainsail which has been folded when the dressing was still wet: the result was the same as happens when a stack of wet hay is erected. When one side of the sails was 'dry', this would only mean that the water had evaporated away; the canvas would remain 'wet' to the touch, because the fish oil would take months to dry out completely. This was the object of dressing the sails: to lubricate from chafe canvas against canvas, or wire or rope against canvas. So the sails remained spread out all night, and I hoped it wouldn't rain. If it did, my only hope was to half-fold all of them in order to prevent the rain from washing off the ochre. I had listened to the weather forecasts; they seemed reasonably safe; it didn't rain that night.

But when, next day, Kester and I turned the sails and dressed their other sides, I knew that in this state any rain could cause maximum harm. Now I could not half-fold, because the side which had 'dried' would not resist a heavy rainfall for at least a week. We completed the job before lunch, and the sun stayed out. After lunch I Stockholm-tarred the ten-inch circumference mainsail headrope and all the bolt ropes; it took me until dusk. That evening it began to rain; it continued all night.

There was only one thing I could do, and I did it. I made up all the sails and covered them with every scrap of material I could find. They were safe enough from the rain, but would they heat up? I paid them a last visit before I went to bed—pushing my hand into the oily folds and trying to decide whether they were warm or hot. The cold drizzle wet my hair; my hands were frozen; my imagination tormented me. I could not decide. I clambered on board *J & M* and washed the red muck off my hands and arms. As I got into bed, Mollie complained sleepily about the sickly stench of the fish oil, but I could only smell burning. I slept badly, dreaming of charred sails and disaster.

The sun, of course, was shining next morning. Another perfect day. Before cooking breakfast I spread the sails. They had not heated; they were not even warm! Oh, how easy life would be if only we could learn not to worry. I spread the sails and admired their colour, and life was good and it was a wonderful morning. I whistled as I cooked breakfast. I was winning. I returned to the land of the living only when Mollie said: 'I wish you'd keep your eye on Sym when you're out there. He's been on those sails again and his paws are covered in red.' Contritely, I said I was sorry. In all honesty I hadn't thought of Mollie, Kester, Sym or Tigger for—well, ever since I had started to fit out! 'The topmast,' I told her, 'I'll house the topmast this morning and get ready for lowering the mast.' 'Well, try and remember to keep an eye on Sym,' Mollie said, and went out to the galley. 'Where's Kes?' I called. 'He's gone to school, of course,' she replied. 'It's Monday.' Damn, I thought, he could have been a help with lowering the topmast.

J & M's 42-foot topmast was fitted with a self-tripping heel bolt or fid. In theory, all one had to do was slacken up the shrouds, forestay and backstays, lead the topmast heel-rope to the mast dolly, and hoist the topmast until it could go no further (there was a metal stop to prevent it from being lifted right through the lower topmast band); then the fid would tip into the vertical position and the topmast could be lowered, or housed. In theory . . .

In practice, as always, it didn't work out like that. I knew from previous experience that the heel of my topmast when wet or damp, fitted just a little too snugly into the heavy metal lower topmast band (which surrounded the mainmast at the hounds and included the spreader- or cross-arm stubs in the assembly). If I lifted the six inches of topmast heel up into this band and it stuck (as it had done once before), then I would have to set up all the shrouds again in order to pull it down out of the band. And as I dared not risk this with the heel fid tripped (because the sudden surge of the spar in free fall might carry away the heel rope), I would be back where I started. So my first job was to grease thoroughly that portion of heel which would enter the lower band. I got my slush bucket and climbed the shrouds.

It is often necessary to lay aloft in any large sailing ship, and many years before I had made quite sure that the task was made as easy and as safe as possible on *J & M*. Rattled down on both sides of the mast with one and a quarter inch lightly-tarred Italian hemp, and with four ash spreaders towards the top across all three shrouds and the backstay shroud, where they nipped together at the hounds, it was very easy to get on to the crossarms. From there to the cap was another climb of about six feet via, on the afterside of the mainmast, the massive hook which carried the forestay, and the eyebolt for the yard tackle (which supported the middle of the spreet). Most barges had ratlines only to starboard—and often they were in a pretty shoddy state too!—but I had long ago discovered the complications which could occur with the topsail (the rigging of which is designed only for dropping to the starboard side of the mainsail), and I knew that my fully-rattled shrouds were a great improvement. Also they enhanced *J & M*'s appearance.

I must admit that I can never lay aloft in any ship without contemplating the scenery and studying the tracery of rigging which is supporting me. I have never scrambled up and up into the vast spider's web which a clipper ship needed to control her driving power, but I always consoled myself with the knowledge that *J & M* was forty per cent of the length of an average clipper ship, and her topmast truck was almost exactly half the height of those seemingly lofty spars. *Cutty*

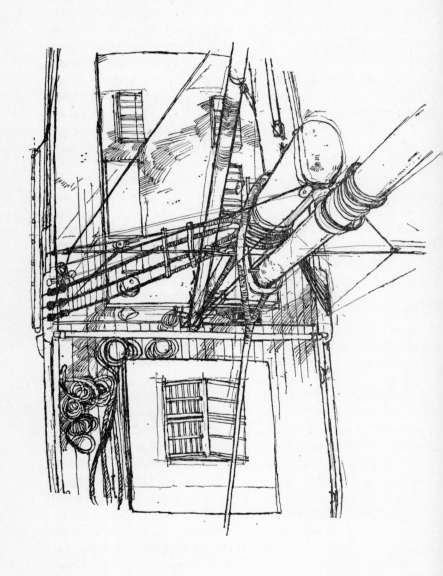

Sark, for example, is 212' 5" long, and her main t'gallant truck is 145' 9" above the deck; *J & M* is 81 feet long and her topmast truck is 72 feet above the deck. I had to admit that I couldn't carry such fancy additional sails as Angel's Wings or Moonrakers, but neither did I have the well-trained and plentiful crew which *Cutty Sark* carried in her heyday. Furthermore, *J & M*'s rig was much more complicated than the simple squaresail, for it is only repetition which creates that spider's web in square rigged ships!

Then again, barges were not all that much slower than those sleek ocean racers. The fastest-ever clipper ship was Donald McKay's *Champion of the Seas*, which had once sailed 465 nautical miles in 24 hours—an average speed of 20 knots; the highest recorded speed in a burst was Donald McKay's *Sovereign of the Seas* which achieved 22 knots on one occasion. Yet barges had often made 12 knots, and such famous racers as *Giralda* and *Sara* were credited with speed bursts in excess of 15 knots. Twice I had driven *J & M* very nearly to her theoretical maximum speed of just over 11 knots—a terrifyingly convincing performance of mighty power in action which I was not anxious to repeat.

I sat on the starboard spreader, feet dangling, and hooked the slush bucket over the 2-inch thick metal arm which supported the hinged spreader (hinged so that either spreader could be lifted into a vertical position by a simple rope hoist— and downhaul—from the deck if the full-width-of-the-ship spreaders, or topmast shrouds, were in danger of fouling other ship's rigging or overhanging obstructions ashore). With my sheath knife I packed grease into the narrow gap between the topmast heel and the 4-inch deep metal band; then I greased the few inches of heel which protruded below the band. I shifted to the other side of the mast and repeated the process there.

The topmast forestay and topmast shrouds were all set up with heavy square-threaded bottle screws. Thanks to a mixture of pump grease and graphite, which I had used for years, there were no problems about freeing the threads. I loosened and unshackled all three quite easily. Then I took the wire topmast heel-rope to the starboard lower mast dolly, rove it round four times, fitted the longest handle for maximum purchase to the upper dolly and wound carefully. The topmast lifted but the fid failed to trip properly. Peering up, I could see that it had very nearly swung into the vertical position, but the weighted end was protruding fractionally and the topmast would not slide down through the band until the fid had completely disappeared into the elongated slot in the heel. I reached for the new length of two inch sisal which I had put by to use as a tail to the wire heel rope, fastened it to the thimble, hitched it to a cleat, removed the handle, and went aloft. A push on the fid and it went into the slot easily. Back to the dolly; unfasten the rope tail.

I eased—e-a-s-e-d—the heel-rope fractionally. With four turns around the drum there would be no danger of a sudden surge as the topmast dropped. Nothing happened. The tail was almost slack. No movement. The bloody heel had jammed in the band in spite of the grease.

Leaving just the tiniest bit of slack on the heel-rope and then cleating the fall, I went to the dangling forestay and pulled gently. Nothing happened. I swung my weight on it. Nothing happened. I checked the heel-rope: the slack had not been taken up. I climbed the rigging and examined the heel: there was no doubt that the previous night's rain had swollen the wood considerably for it filled the band tightly and grease oozed from the compression. I climbed down, cursed, and began to set up the topmast shroud bottle screws—these I knew would drag the heel down.

But, of course, the topmast was now some six inches higher than before, and even with the threads fully extended both bottle screws could not be shackled to their chainplates. One would, because the now-whippy topmast could easily be bent, but I had to find an additional shackle for the other. I started to tighten them, using my 18-inch marline spike. Silently the topmast crept downwards and took up the slack of the heel-rope.

Once again I unshackled the topmast shrouds. Once again I unfastened the heel-rope and eased it around the dolly. This time, at last, the topmast slid down the front of the mast until the heel was just above the mast-case. I lashed the heel to the mast, flicked the heel-rope coils off the dolly, unbent the rope tail, cleared up and restowed all the gear and equipment which I had used, and . . . then it was lunchtime.

And Sym *had* been on the sails again. . . .

'You might have kept an eye on him,' Mollie said. . . .

'Oh, let him bloody roll on them if he wants to,' I mumbled angrily. . . .

There was the topmast rigging to check. . . .

I had examined the lower sections as I coiled them; now, after lunch, I checked each one as I climbed the ratlines—first to starboard, then to port. Then I clambered up the last six feet of the mainmast and sat, facing forward, on the cap. At crutch level the conglomeration of five eye splices, resting on a stout metal band (to which was shackled: forward, two feet of chain and a single block for the staysail halliard; aft, a large single-sheave swivel block for the topsail halliard), with eight metal topmast hoops jammed between these and the cap band, made close examination of the splices difficult. I stood up on the cap, steadying myself by hanging on to the scarlet pole, and the round golden ball of the truck was just above eye level; into the truck was screwed the three foot six inch metal staff which supported the frame to which the 'bob' or flag was sewn; a few remnants of bunting were still attached to this frame—all that was left after five years of weathering. I adjusted the jaws of the 18-inch Stilson which I had carried aloft for this job, and unscrewed the staff—lowering it, and the Stilson, to the deck on a length of codline. Then, still standing on the cap, I lifted each eyesplice off over the truck so that I could examine it properly.

Masts which are supported with thick wires must, of necessity, always be rigged the same way. If the eyesplices of the main rigging were fitted over the hounds in the wrong order, then the thick wadding of parcelling and serving around each eye could cause a difference of as much as ten inches to the length of the shroud at deck level. The order is: shrouds, backstays, forestay—always port on first. Actually, a barge has an oddment, the stanliff, which supports the heel of the spreet; this is the very first eyesplice to fit over the hounds— followed by the port shrouds, the starboard shrouds, the port backstays, the starboard backstays, the main forestay. The topmast is rigged in the same way.

So, standing on the cap, I bent down and lifted the topmast forestay up the pole, off over the truck, and slipped the eyesplice on to my left arm, repeating the process until I had cleared all five eyesplices. Then I lowered myself gingerly to sit once again on the cap, lashed four of the splices to a topsail hoop and began my inspection with the port topmast shroud—which was, of course, the first to refit over the truck.

I had thought that this inspection would only need to be cursory—more as a salve to my worrying than anything else. As I plucked at the bleached and rotting spunyarn serving on the first eyesplice I realised that all five would have to be re-parcelled and re-served—and that meant lowering the lot down to the deck! Would I ever finish this laborious fitting-out?

By 2000 hours, working steadily in the fo'c's'le under a hissing Tilley (which supplied warmth as well as light), I completed the work. Four splices were O.K., the fifth was badly rusted. Now I had to find some suitable wire to replace the topmast forestay—the longest single length of rigging on the barge.

I went outside into the field to make up the sails for the night—just in case it rained—and I craved and craved for a release from the tension. If only somebody would turn up tomorrow and make an offer for *J & M*. . . . If only somebody would appreciate the unique possibilities which *J & M* offered—a film, television, anything. . . . If only I could make some money quickly. . . . If only . . . But *J & M* lay quietly in her berth, the golden glow from the saloon skylights faintly illuminating her now-tangled rigging, and there were no answers to my prayers in the wilderness of the night.

I dreamt of disaster: of wild seas, of frantic winds, of desperate leaks, of cracking spars, of tangled rigging. And in my dream of despair I clawed my way aft into the after cabin, scrabbled up the floorboards, and there found a brand-new coil of wire. . . .

The next morning it was there—not the result of a miracle, but merely my subconscious working, as it had to work, overtime. That coil had lain there for eight or nine years, absolutely forgotten. It was one of the many oddments which I had collected in the early days, stowed under the cabin sole because it was an awkward size to stow anywhere else. It was the right circumference ($1\frac{3}{4}''$) and material: plow-steel. Was it long enough? I drove a wooden peg into the ground ashore, stretched the old topmast forestay and measured the new against it. There was twenty feet to spare! And—joy of joys—one end already had a thimble spliced into it.

Plow-steel is an ugly wire to splice. It is rock-hard, inflexible and very nearly impossible to handle in a confined area. Given a roomy work-bench, a tough vice, and overhead space for feeding the wire vertically to the vice, I could have coped easily enough; as it was, I had to complete that soft-eye splice by hand. It took me over three hours. Three-and-a-half tucks, well-hammered into tapering neatness, greased, then parcelled and served—good for at least ten years, maybe more.

That afternoon the topmast shrouds, backstays, and new forestay were back in their correct positions.

A barge's mast, complete with all rigging and sails, is designed so that it can all be lowered quickly by one man—whilst, if necessary, the barge is sailing. The object was to enable barges to 'shoot' bridges, generally on the London river. Usually a third man, called the 'huffler' was taken on board for this hazardous performance; his job was to lower away smartly whilst the skipper steered and the mate stood to one side to watch and warn as required. On the wind, and only with a favourable tide, the skipper would time his approach so that his barge was on the most advantageous **tack**

before luffing. Seconds before hitting the arch, the huffler
would fleet the stayfall wire smoothly around the previously
water-soaked windlass barrel and the five tons or so of
mast and gear would fall backwards like a toppling Tower
of Pisa. Just before it hit the deck, the huffler would check the
stayfall. This was the moment of greatest danger: if he checked
too late, the gear *would* hit the deck, or the 'bounce' caused by
the sudden jolt of stopping five tons from free-falling would
cause it to hit; if he checked too soon, the barge would be under
the arch before he could release more fall—and the gear would
snag the bridge with disastrous results. It was, as can be
imagined, a fine art.

The stayfall—twenty-five fathoms of 2-inch flexible steel
wire—is rove through two enormous treble-sheave metal
blocks at the stemhead. Sometimes these blocks are covered
with canvas in order to preserve the wire which passes through
them from weathering. The stayfall itself is parcelled and
served over some twenty feet and is normally stowed, via a
hawse pipe in the deck alongside the starboard bitts, coiled in
the fo'c's'le—the tarred serving protecting it from the weather
'tween stayfall blocks and hawse pipe.

Since we used *J & M* more as a houseboat than a sea-going
vessel, I had made a habit of removing the stayfall blocks whenever we were obviously berthed for a long period, and replacing them with a large square-threaded bottle-screw which
I had found in a scrap yard soon after we moved on board.
It was a bit of a struggle to exchange blocks for bottle-screw,
or vice versa, but I was sure that the effort was justified:
blocks and stayfall were still in as-new condition.

So now I set a tackle to the main forestay, immediately
over the fo'c's'le hatch, with a rolling hitch; broke out the
stayfall blocks and tackle from the forepeak (with much
grunting, struggling, puffing and swearing, for it was awkward
in shape and well over two hundred pounds in weight), and
hoisted them on deck; took the housed topmast forestay fall
to the main windlass and cranked it taut; set up the main
runners to the rolling-wang chain plates; clapped a tackle

on the main forestay and set it up as taut as possible against the fores'l tack eyebolt in the stemhead; slackened the bottle-screw, unbolted and removed it; bolted the upper stayfall block to the forestay, then the lower block to the stemhead; rove the stayfall thrice around the windlass; removed the tackle holding the main forestay, and the topmast forestay from the windlass; cranked the windlass until the stayfall blocks were set up; unhooked the main runners and re-set them up in their usual positions. Time: the rest of the daylight hours of that afternoon and half the next morning; I spent the other half setting up the third new lanyard.

At lunch, Mollie said despairingly: 'Sym has been on those damn sails again. I do wish you'd keep an eye on him.'

I asked, tensely, how the hell I could keep watching Sym when it was as much as I could do to keep a watchful eye on all the hazards which I was tackling? I recognised tension and I understood apprehension; goodness knows, I wanted to avoid dissension. Lonely, unhappy, worried, without a solitary glimmer of light in the black void of the future, I went back on deck to my endless chores. I already knew that I was entering a black period, when luck would be as fickle as the williwaws which dither ahead of an advancing storm, but I had learned often enough in the past that the blackness can only be penetrated by advancing, and that faith and hope are of little use without a fierce determination to press on—regardless.

Now I was cross; now I was beginning to hate. Oh, you bitch, I thought; and I wasn't thinking about Mollie! Oh you lousy, bastard cow!

But hating is a waste of energy and I could neither afford the time nor the luxury. I was winning—slowly. The long plod of the preparations would come to an end; then the battle to sail south would start.

Step by step: when you are alone, and an unavoidable battle has to be fought, you must accept the rough with the smooth and keep going.

I stood by *J & M*'s wheel and rested my hand on the

uppermost spoke. The sun was warm, and a faint breeze came from astern. Instinctively I looked aloft, but with the topmast housed and the bob removed my barge could no longer pass me a message from the wind. With an effort I evolved my next chore and thrust myself to getting on with it.

Oh, the loneliness of command!

5. INTO THE MILL-RACE

I have often wondered whether others suffer as I do from a singlemindedness of purpose which obliterates everything and everybody from thought and action except those items which concern the venture in progress. I cannot believe that I am unique, but I have yet to meet a person who mirrors my self-centred, seemingly objectionable total involvement during an adventure.

Uncle Fred and Hopalong had played their brief parts in the enterprise and had been forgotten. Mollie and Kester flickered in and out of my limited vision and were remembered only because they were a recurring familiarity. Sym was doggishly sympathetic on occasions, but Tigger was always gloriously aloof—I suspect that he and I had much in common, although we never spoke about it.

The plodding labour of fitting out *J & M* was delicately counterbalanced against how long my original £150 capital would last. Thus time, my limit of freedom, was measured by money—as always was, and always will be the case.

To strike a balance of success out of a profit and loss of imponderables is an accountant's nightmare. Theoretical skill is useless; practical ability is only a small percentage of the assets. Total involvement in the enterprise, to the exclusion of all else, may save premature bankruptcy—may, not will—but it will never guarantee more than that, although at this stage every penny of credit will help. Then with the imponderables will come some brief perks of luck which, if checked into the account as all petty cash should be, may avoid a deficit. It is a frightening game, this balancing of accounts.

I awoke to the prompting of the conscious part of my mind

to find that the afternoon had slipped away. Long shadows and a dipping sun chilled the air. Yet the time had not been wasted. When there is nobody with whom you can argue, then you must discourse with yourself. I felt refreshed. Once again I had accentuated the point to myself that there was no alternative to what I was doing, and that so far I had done everything correctly, at the best possible speed, with a minimum of cash expenditure. The books were still balancing. I hoped there would be no more shocks like that topmast forestay.

The next few days were lost in a conglomeration of pottering—frigging in the rigging is an apt description. Like a bumble bee after nectar, I investigated block after block, shackle after shackle, splice after splice; with oil-can, grease-tin, spunyarn, whipping twine, knife, King Dick and marline spike to hand, I could not fail to recall the joyful chorus of the barrack-room ditty, ' 'twas on the good ship "Venus". . .':

'Frigging in the rigging.
Frigging in the rigging.
Frigging in-n-n-n the rigging!
There's f—— all else to do.'

So clear were the memories of mess parties in which I had yelled this bawdy song, that I flitted through the routine rigging chores in a haze of retrospect which concealed the procession of hours. Over and over again the chorus beat through my mind; repeatedly individual voices chanted the filthy verses.

'Frigging in-n-n-n the rigging!
There's f—— all else to do.'

There *was* nothing else to do. This checking and repairing and block-oiling and greasing had to be completed before I could lift the sails on board (with all the associated confusion), and then lower the mast. It was a long and monontonous job.

Coupled with the work, came the pleasurable activity of replacing old running rigging with new rope. Main runners, tops'l halliard, tops'l backstays—no, I had renewed these the previous autumn and the 2-inch sisal was as good as new when I inspected it—stays'l halliard, spreader lifts and downhauls (I had some 1-inch cotton rope spare for these—quite adequate

for the job), mizzen sheet, mizzen stanliff, yard tackle. . . .
My fingers, which had been hardened by sewing and wire-
splicing, re-suffered from the multitudinous duties involved
in splicing and whipping coarse sisal; in spite of this, I liked the
job, since it is as much a joy to clothe a sailing ship with new
running rigging as it must be for a couturier to dress a beautiful
woman.

And so at last I was ready for the sails.

I allowed myself no pause for despair this time, and I gave
Mollie only the briefest notice.

'I'm bringing the sails on board tomorrow,' I told her, and
I had no need to say more. She knew, as I did, the difficulties
involved.

Our 'front door' entrance which served us when our barge
was a houseboat would now be dismantled—more or less
for the duration of the projected voyage. The fore-and-aft
10-foot long flap on the starboard side of the main hatch
could be propped open without any trouble, but the canvas
covered framework which supported the front door was
complicated to erect, and was not designed for use in connec-
tion with the sailing part of our lives. There was a stowage
for the framework, canvas, and door behind the companion-
way (the paraffin fridge was in a tiled compartment directly
under the top platform of the companionway), and once the
long flap was lowered the only entrances were via the after
cabin or the fo'c's'le hatch. These vertical companionways
were not as easy to negotiate as the houseboat staircase.

'Well, you'll have to wear trousers,' I told Mollie grumpily;
then I relented my mood—as I had on so many thousands of
previous similar occasions—and added: 'It won't be for long,
darling. I'll get the sails on board as quickly as I can, drop the
gear, bend on the mains'l, arrange with one of the motor
barges for a tow to Ferriby, and then we can get the mast up.
There's no point in hoisting here 'cause I'll only have to lower
away again to tow through the bridges. Give it a week.'

Mollie said: 'A week! And all the mess from those sails!
I *hate* going into town in trousers.'

EE

Kester said, unsympathetically: 'Are you going to start tomorrow, Nobby?'

I nodded.

I suppose that, deep down, Mollie was as disturbed as I at our, and *J & M*'s prospects. Instinctively, womanlike, she was registering her uncertainty of mind. But although I recognised her protest, I could do nothing to assuage it; the work had to go on.

Before the mainsail could be dragged and lifted on board, it had first to be rigged. I measured new against old 2-inch sisal inner and outer, and upper and lower brails, and rove them off. I fitted the main brails, splicing the last length of the 3-inch Indian hemp through the double cringles on the leach to make the strop which holds the brails in position. The sail had to be turned once before this job was completed, but I had Kester to give a hand now—he had left his school for the Easter holidays, and for always.

Now the sail had to be folded neatly within the loops of the brails, with the leach and luff exposed on opposite sides; then the brails were drawn as tight as possible, coiled, and lashed into position; finally the mainsail was made up in stops. The elongated red slug, cocooned in stops and coils of wire and rope, was over fifty feet long and probably weighed about one and a quarter tons with the fresh dressing and all the gear. It lay about thirty yards from *J & M*'s deck, with an 8-foot gap between barge and river bank, and the 10-foot high sea-wall to negotiate.

Just as the stayfall blocks and tackle were replaced with a bottle-screw whenever *J & M* became a houseboat, so was the mainsail unbent and taken ashore for stowing. But the spreet of a barge is supported solely by the headrope of the mainsail, which is usually of wire—although *J & M*'s mainsail was so old that it still had a 10-inch hempen headrope. So when the mainsail was removed, something was needed to hold up the spreet, and in the early days of ownership I had spliced, parcelled, and served throughout the whole length, a replacement headrope of $2\frac{1}{2}$-inch wire. Similarly, I had not wasted the new wangs to the weather, but had bent on the old wangs for her five-year rest at Brigg.

So now I fastened a snatch-block to her starboard wang and slackened the port wang until the spreet pointed over the river bank. Using the dolly wire, I rove it through a block in the stem-head, as I had done when I dragged the mainsail into the field, through the snatch-block attached to the wang, and from there to the headrope of the mainsail. I wrapped the tail around the windlass barrel, and began to crank. With Kester checking the slow progress of the heavy sail along the ground we got the peak of the headrope to the top of the sea-wall.

Although the pull from the peak of the spreet was adequate to match the upward slope of the sea-wall on the far side, the deadweight of the sail was putting too much strain on the three-quarter inch dolly wire. Something would have to be done to ease the load. I slackened off the wire.

Kester and I took the floorboards out of the skiff, and with levers we lifted the heaviest part of the mainsail and slid the two floorboards, upside-down, underneath. Two large cylindrical rope fenders were positioned in a similar manner. I tried the windlass again; the strain was noticeably lessened. We gained another fifteen feet, but by now the peak of the mainsail had reached the snatch-block on the wang. I slackened off the wire.

I re-fastened the dolly wire tail around the mainsail some twenty feet from the peak, repositioned the skiff floorboards and fender rollers, and cranked again. But now the weight of the sail which was already over the sea-wall was altering the angle of pull, and this time I gained only ten feet before the creaking of J & M's rigging and the strumming of the dolly wire warned me that the strain was too great. I slackened off yet again.

Kester and I tried physically to move the red slug which was draped across the sea-wall, but it was as immovable as a dead hippopotamus would have been in the same position.

'We'll have to shift the wire to the skirt end,' I told Kester, 'reposition the floorboards and fenders, and try again.'

We did. It was a hard struggle.

It took a working day to rig, make up, and crank the mainsail from the field to the river bank. It took another day to dismantle the entrance door, and lift the mainsail, section by section, across the 8-foot gap between bank and barge, using the double-burton on the spreet, and finally to stretch the sail out along the starboard main hatch and after deck in the correct position to bend it to the spreet when it was lowered. By comparison, the foresail, topsail and mizzen were easy—yet they took another two days before they were individually rigged and dragged into position on board.

The decks were now a shambles of red-ochred sails. There was worse to follow—the mast had to be lowered.

I removed the two holding-bolts from the open after-side of the mast-case, unfastened the stopper on the stayfall whilst Kester held the tail which lead from the three turns around the windlass barrel, told Kester to stand on the port deck just forward of the main horse (where he was comparatively safe if anything parted, yet he could see everything and shout a warning if a snag occurred), remembered belatedly that I had not removed the galley chimney and switched positions with Kester to unbolt the stays and lay the 8-foot length of 5-inch diameter asbestos pipe on the side deck (Mollie complained and stated categorically that lunch would be ruined—but what else could I do?), double-checked that all the skylights were closed (Mollie said that she was being suffocated—which I did not doubt as the Rayburn could not clear poisonous fumes without the draught of a tallish chimney), told Sym who was complaining at the foot of the after-cabin companionway to stay there and be quiet, changed places again with Kester, and then, at last, slowly fed the stayfall around the barrel. We were not shooting a bridge and I lowered slowly— marvelling, as I did every time I dropped the gear, that this trick was performed regularly in the old days, and that it had been completed in a matter of seconds.

Just before the spreet grounded on the main hatch, I swapped places with Kester and told him to fleet the stayfall about a foot or so when I shouted. 'There's not all that much strain, and you can hold it easily,' I said, and left him with the first real responsibility he had ever had on board.

I ducked under and climbed over the sagging rigging, and dragged a heavy baulk of timber to bridge the gap between the starboard quarter rail and the after-cabin coachroof. Then I sat on the coachroof, braced my back against the steering shaft with my feet on the free-swinging spreet, and shouted to Kester: 'Lower away!' As the spreet thumped to rest on the timber support I shoved with all my might, and managed to keep it far enough to starboard to give access along the after deck.

We changed places again.

As the mast dropped lower and lower, Kester stood amidships by the main horse with the mast prop in position. This was a 5-foot, 2-inch thick plank, specially strapped and notched to receive and hold the weight of the mast—rather than leave it straining at the stayfall, or, much worse, lowering it to deck level from where it would be impossible to lift without first using a jack of some sort, either under the mast or the forestay.

He positioned the prop exactly right: the mast was secure. I made fast the stayfall to the starboard bow bollards and lashed it with spunyarn against accidental release, set up the galley chimney, opened some skylights, gave Sym a rearside shove to help him climb the ladder, and then sat on the grounded spreet and surveyed the confusion which we had just created.

Of course, I hadn't laid out the mainsail far enough aft. Every bloody time I had rigged *J & M* I had made this miscalculation. The tip of the spreet extended over the taffrail by about six feet, and the job of slipping the large eye spliced in the peak of the 10-inch headrope over the end of the spreet was made a little easier if there was plenty of slack in the rest of the mainsail. This meant that the mainsail had to be laid out on the coachroofs and deck further aft than at first appeared necessary.

Kester wanted to help, but I sent him away to play with a friend. He did not have the weight or the muscle power to be of any use, and it was better that he kept clear whilst I grunted, sweated, strained, heaved, pushed and swore that mainsail another three feet aft, broke out the 'best' wangs and shackled them to the steel ring around the joggle, and then forced the headrope eye over the spreet, hammering it down with a large wooden mallet. I shackled the topsail sheet block to the upper side of the steel ring, replaced the two rolling wang softeye-splices and nailed them in position, and that completed the work at the spreet end. It took nearly five hours with only a break for lunch during which Mollie complained that Sym was treading the red ochre everywhere.

Over the next five days, sometimes with Kester's help

sometimes without, I chained the mainsail throat to the mast collar, shackled the luff to the jackstay, rove the brails through their respective blocks and fairleads, bent the foresail to the hanks on the forestay, rigged the foresail halliard, rigged a new staysail halliard, bent the topsail headstick to the peak of the topsail (nine feet in length, of heavy pitchpine), rigged a new topsail sheet, rigged the topsail halliard and newly-rove tackle, rigged the mizzen and then lowered it on deck ready for towing through the bridges. . . .

The confusion on deck was now absolute. Twice it rained, and the scuppers ran red with ochre. Sym resembled a canine Red Indian and even Tigger failed to avoid contact. Mollie said nothing more—an ominous sign. I had to organise a tow quickly. . . .

The pace was increasing through the pressure of circumstances. This is the weakness in any adventure. During the early stages only money worries had enforced action; now my action had sublimated reactions which enforced further action on my part. From the trickle of necessity I had flowed comparatively easily via rivulet and stream into a torrent of turmoil; now we were trapped in a mill-race from which escape would be impossible until we had passed under the shadow of the multi-bladed waterwheel which was churning inexorably somewhere just ahead. Only then could the mad pace slacken.

6. ADDITIONAL CREW

The River Ancholme was straightened into a canal by French prisoners during the Napoleonic Wars. Since then, large numbers of Humber keels, sloops, and other long-forgotten types of vessel had traded up the canalised river to Brigg and to the many farms and hamlets which lined its 20-mile length. I had seen photos, taken in the early nineteen-hundreds, showing queues of craft delivering sugar beet to the Brigg factory and awaiting cargoes of sugar for transport to the Midlands or to ships at Hull. All of those vessels which jammed the Ancholme from bank to bank, stretching away into the distance and out of the photos, were sail-driven or horse-drawn; now half a dozen or so motor-barges were all that were left—delivering fuel to the storage tanks which blocked the view immediately to the east of New Bridge.

These steel tankers were specially built for the job, and their crews were mostly an unlovely motley crowd who were neither seamen nor ex-sailormen. Keeping to schedule, and thus ensuring maximum pay, was their sole interest, and they bashed their tin-can vessels mercilessly and continuously in the pursuit of this unhappy living. They were tram-drivers, not seamen: they ran along fixed grooves in the rivers and frequently left damage in their wake when anybody had the temerity to block their path. They motored at one speed: flat out, with stern sucked down and bows high when the going was shallow and narrow, as it was in the Ancholme. Yachts moored alongside anywhere on their many routes would rear and plunge and smash and crash as the tidal-wave boiled along the river banks, but protests from owners, and even from river authorities who worried about scouring

72

effects, were ignored. 'We have to bloody work 'ard for our pay, mate,' was the sort of excuse they produced, 'an' we 'aven't got f——ing time to fart about with the throttle for every bloody tin-pot yot we see. Let 'em put the pissing things somewhere else; we've got work to do.'

When *J & M* first arrived at Brigg, I required just one experience of these bulldozing tactics before I exploded. I realised that against such appalling ignorance it would be of little use to complain; I resorted, therefore, to castigating them and their bloody-mindedness.

'Call yourself f——ing seamen,' I raged, 'your fathers would f——ing turn in their f——ing graves if they knew how you handled those f——ing iron-pots. What you f——ing need is some f——ing instructions on how to f——ing wipe your f——ing arses.'

'Now look 'ere, mate . . .' said the shifty-eyed 'captain' who had first aroused my wrath—but as far as I was concerned he had already lost the argument; conciliatory anxiety was already apparent in his voice and demeanour.

'Don't you f——ing "mate" me,' I bawled. 'You go f——ing charging up and down this f——ing river like a f——ing bull in a f——ing china shop, causing f——ing damage all over the f——ing place, and then you f——ing try to f——ing "mate" me.'

By now he looked slightly dazed. I had discovered many years before that constant repetition of the adjective most used by a certain type of 'working' class was the finest weapon to use against such people when attacking hard. The reason is not difficult to understand, for familiarity blanks thought, and *they* used the four-letter word frequently enough amongst themselves not to notice it. But when f——ing pearls of f——ing wisdom poured from the lips of a so-called white-collar worker. . . .

'Look, mister,' he said, 'I didn't realise we would cause any trouble to your barge. I thought she was so big that our wash wouldn't move 'er. I'll tell you what. Next time we go on the yard, I'll bring you some warps to replace those we snapped—an' anything else I can find.'

And, of course, immediately he backed down like this I began to feel a bit of a heel for losing my temper. But my tirade worked. From that day, every tanker skipper cut his throttle well before he came up to where *J & M* lay, and did not open up again until he had passed. I doubt if they altered their tactics elsewhere, but that was not my problem. We were 'mates', and we stayed that way.

In 1952 *J & M* had been towed up to Brigg by the owner of a converted lifeboat whom I had met in the pub which lies alongside the South Ferriby locks. Money was not tight then, and I had given him a fiver for the nine-mile tow. Now I had to organise a tow back to Ferriby—preferably free—and so I had waited for the arrival of the tanker skipper whom I considered was the least split-arse, and therefore the safest to trust with the responsibility.

'Yes, sure we'll give you a tow,' he said. 'Do you want to come with us this time, or on the next trip?'

'When will you be back?' I asked.

'Three days time.'

And so the tow was settled.

Three days, I thought, would give us ample time to take in stores. Mollie was not so sure.

'How long are we going to be at sea?' she asked. 'There's Sym's food', (he was at that time consuming twelve pounds of raw meat a week, plus biscuits and anything else going), and Tigger will need a sackful of earth for his tray. And where's Sym going to go—he's too big for a tray! The fridge isn't large enough to keep Sym's food and ours. And what about washing the clothes? And baths? Have we got enough money to buy food?' And then, irrationally: 'I'll be damned glad to get to Ferriby so that you can get the mast up and the decks clear.'

But she did her job, as I knew she would, magnificently. Mollie hated *J & M*, but she appreciated our commitment to the venture as much as I did. I bought a hundredweight of potatoes and a gross of eggs cheaply from a friendly farmer; Mollie, with Kester helping, brought the rest of the stores on board. She solved the Sym food problem by discovering a source of 7-pound tins of dog-meat, made in Eire. She dhobied madly to ensure that water would be saved on the trip. On the last night at Brigg we all bathed—that, too, was her idea.

On the morning of the third day, Kester and I filled all the water tanks and then coiled up the 200 yards of hose. I dropped the manhole cover for the last time over our tap on the embankment on the west side of New Bridge, and looked back across the river to where *J & M* lay, her decks untidy, her appearance desolate in spite of the morning sun. Already the landmark of five years had gone: the lofty topmast, the fluttering bob, the canted spreet—these had shown her presence around the flat fenlands much more than her massive hull. Now they were gone, forever; in a few hours the river bank too would be naked.

Our tug arrived on schedule, discharged, turned round in the small bay made for this purpose just off *J & M*'s bows, and

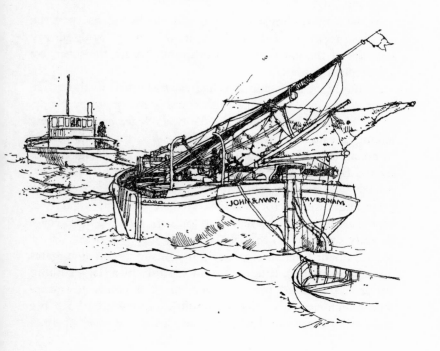

took our best warp. She waited, engine idling, whilst Kester
and I released the bow and stern lines and struggled to get the
heavy gangplank inboard as *J & M* drifted gently into the
stream. I clambered across the cluttered deck and flipped the
locking fid off the back of the wheel, waved to the skipper of
our tug, and prepared to shoot New Bridge. Sym barked
ecstatically; Tigger clung to the mainsail with extended claws
and stared with round eyes at the receding shore; Mollie
stood by me at the helm and thought her own thoughts;
Kester crouched at the bow, to be first under the low bridge;
I spun the wheel this way and that, trying to straighten my ship
so that she met the bridge exactly in the centre of the arch—
I knew that the clearance was very little and that there was no
margin for error.

And so we left Brigg as we came, without fuss. A few people
watched us pass under New Bridge; some waved. We had
paid all that we owed and departed quietly. It had been a good
place to visit.

As we slipped almost silently down the Ancholme, past the
rapidly greening fields and under the many bridges, my
anxieties of the last few weeks evaporated with the sheer joy
of movement at last.

I thought of all I, and we, had accomplished in those five
years. I had moved north to become a flying instructor to
grade potential pilots for the Korean War, and we were
leaving because another war, Suez, had virtually eliminated
all possibilities of continuing my training as a road aggregates
expert. Between these wars, and these extremes of jobs, I had
worked as a sign-painter, weighbridgeman, wire-splicer
(including three factories and a circus), barman, sugar beet
hoer, rigger, coalman, surveyor (on a £1,250,000 project—
the only surveyor on the job), quantity surveyor, lorry driver
and salesman; I had also spent six months in a road aggregates
laboratory; made a time and motion study of a slag-crushing
business; organized my own version of a youth adventure
club (which certainly achieved results), and started a boat hire
business on the Ancholme. They had been years well-spent.

Soon, we passed under the concrete bridge which carried the 21-inch water pipeline across the Ancholme, which I had helped to build in 1955. I remembered the difficulties of locating firm foundations for the piles and the vast quantities of cement which the borings had consumed, of the problems of running sand, bog oak (we had discovered a forest of almost-petrified oaks), and access—particularly the latter, because fenmen are, and always will be, against interlopers, and will recall with pride such adventures as those of Hereward the Wake to stress their regret for their loss of freedom. Theirs was the last stronghold of independence in England to concede to the rule of a central government; from what I had discovered during my many adventures amongst them, they still regretted this decision.

We tied up alongside the wharf at South Ferriby; the tow had taken just over an hour and a half. Within minutes cars began to park on the greensward of the wharf, and people began to peer. It was just after five, and we were collecting the homeward bound workers who used the Humber-side route.

One of the penalties of living afloat—particularly if the vessel is reasonably unique—is the interest which one un-avoidably creates. We had had many years' experience. It was as if we were custodians of an Ancient Monument, because we soon discovered that the public regarded our ship as their property. We called them 'gongoozlers', an appropriate description which we learned from L. T. C. Rolt's wonderful book about canal barges, *Narrow Boat*.

An early enlightening episode was when we anchored off Chalkwell beach (Westcliff-on-Sea) and allowed *J & M* to dry out on the hard so that we could show her off to relatives. They walked out on the hard, and clambered aboard via a ladder over the side. We were having tea—about a dozen of us—when I heard noises in the passageway outside the saloon door. 'Must be some more friends,' I said, and went out to greet them. But, no, I didn't recognise the young fellow or the girl who were peering down the passage towards our bedroom. To my question, he replied: 'We just came to have a look. My girl wanted to use a toilet, so we thought we'd see if there was one here.'

On another voyage in this area, we sailed into Bell Wharf at Old Town, Leigh-on-Sea. We were, incidentally, the last *sailing* barge to do so, because the old crane was dismantled, and the wharf opened to the public shortly afterwards, so it was finished forever as a trading wharf. One day I discovered that our barge skiff was missing, and after a couple of hours—just before the tide left us—it was brought back by a cockler crew. (They used to be called bawleymen, but they lost their title when they abandoned the magnificent sailing bawleys for motorised cocklers.)

'Where did you find it?' I asked, preparing to offer profuse thanks.

'Tied up 'ere,' he mumbled ungraciously. 'I only borrowed it to put off to me cockler.'

'Don't you ever bother to ask permission before you take a boat?' I said pointedly, beginning to lose my temper at this casual, and rude approach.

''Course not,' was his scornful reply, 'we 'elp each other round 'ere. Besides,' he added, 'barges is public property.' And he meant it.

So we were well-acquainted with gongoozlers! Mollie hated them, Kester liked showing off to them, Sym showed his teeth at them, Tigger and I ignored them. They were never put off by any of these tactics. They materialised; they stood; they watched; they commented: 'Look,' they would say, peering down the companion-way, 'she's making tea now. There's a big stove down there. She's putting cups and saucers and plates through a window-thing. They must eat in there. Coo, in'nt nice. . . .'

It was a quiet, still, late afternoon. . . .

'Come on, Kes,' I said. 'Let's hoist the gear.'

I cut free the tail lashing of the stayfall from the starboard bow bollard, and wound it around the windlass barrel—tucking the end under the standing part so that it would jamb when

I commenced winding. I shut all the skylights, removed the galley chimney, stationed Kester to catch the mast-prop as it fell away, and then tried the windlass. I could barely turn it— even when I used the maximum leverage of the second socket in the handle. Two clunks of the pawls were sufficient to remove the mast-prop, but I doubted whether Kester and I had sufficient weight or muscle-power to hoist the gear all the way. 'Take the other handle,' I called to Kester after he had laid the prop on the deck. We tried together—him to port, handle up; me to starboard, handle down.

Clank . . . clank . . . barely, clank . . .

We couldn't do it. Mollie would have to help.

And then a voice said: 'Here, Nobby, we'll give you a hand,' and I looked round to see Felton and a stranger stepping on board.

'Thanks a lot, Felton,' I said gratefully. 'Here, Kes, you come this side with me, and they can take the other handle.' Facing each other in pairs on each handle the labour was immediately lightened to little more than a mangling session.

As the spreet began to lift to the tug of the mainsail headrope, I called a halt to check that the two steel rings chained to the muzzle, which held the spreet alongside the mast, were securely round the joggle at the foot of the spreet, and that the stanliff which was shackled to the steel band, and now prevented the spreet from sliding forward, was also shipshape. Then I walked around the deck making sure that standing and running rigging and sails were not fouling skylights, coachroof edges or anything else. I took Kester off the windlass and stationed him to port by the main-horse, in the 'safe' watching position. Then we recommenced cranking.

Slowly, bit by bit, with the untidy folds of the unbrailed mainsail tipping pockets of rainwater in sudden gushes, with dead grass and hunks of dried earth dropping and with sudden slithers as sail or rigging were freed, the mainmast rose to the vertical position.

'That's it,' I called.

I slipped the two locking bolts into the mast-case, and

screwed up the nuts. I broke out the two double-double 2½-inch manila-rove wang falls, shackled them to the gently swinging wangs and made fast. I cranked the main brail winch until the mainsail leech was drawn tight to the throat, and hove in the inners and outers to their cleats: the after shrouds to port and starboard, and the middles and lowers to their respective cleats on each side of the mast-case.

Kester swept all the muck off the decks.

I made up the foresail into the harbour-stow unique to barges—winding the downhaul round and round from luff to clew, and then hoisting the tapered result three-quarters up the forestay, with the clew chained to the wooden fore-horse, and the bowline clove-hitched to the stanliff to prevent the chain sheet from rattling.

In the meantime, Felton and his friend had raised the mizzen by its forestay tackle, and made fast the mizzen brails and mizzen boom topping-lift and sheet; at Mollie's indignant shouted request they replaced the galley chimney.

J & M was beginning to look like a sailing ship once again. I paused from my labours and looked aloft. Tomorrow I had to shackle on the mainsheet, hoist the topmast, bend on the top-sail, unreeve the stayfall from the windlass, hank on the stay-sail. . . . Then there were all the gaps in the planking which I had to stop up, and we needed a new bob, and I had to see the lockkeeper about locking out. . . .

'Come on,' I said to Felton as I lifted the main companion-way hatch and propped it open, 'introduce me to your friend, and come and have a cup of tea. And thanks for all your help.'

I had met Felton Mixford when I was a weighbridgeman at the British Sugar Corporation factory at Brigg. Like Hopa-long, he was operating alone with his own lorry—and like so many owners of new lorries within sixty or so miles of Mablethorpe, he had achieved financial success as a result of the disastrous floods which swept across the low-lying fen districts in 1953, and nearly eliminated some coastal towns such as Mablethorpe. It's an ill wind . . .

Felton had known that *J & M* was my barge, and he had

introduced himself at the weighbridge by loaning me books about sailing ships. He was one of those enthusiasts who ship-spot with all the zest of youngsters after trains and car numbers, or amateur naturalists watching birds. So, of course, I invited him along to see *J & M*. We had discovered then that he was not entirely what he seemed—a self-employed lorry driver. As a matter of fact, that is just about all we did discover because he told us very little about what he had done in the past.

He was, I would say, some ten years older than me, and a good two inches taller. Compared with my beefiness (even although I did not have an ounce of superfluous fat left on my body after six weeks of fitting out), he was skinny: lanky-lean—but hard, hard as nails physically. He was a good listener, but a poor talker—unless one talked ships, or aircraft. This was surprising, because his exotic name seemed to imply greater horizons. I never found out where he was born, but he certainly didn't come from Lincolnshire.

His friend, Len did. Len was about my height, and half as heavy again. Fat, jolly, and evidently content with his lot, he was the sort of forty-year-old who would have a brood of half-a-dozen or so kids; in fact, he had five. The only similarity between Felton and Len was that they were both ardent ship-spotters.

Len's father had been skipper of one of the last of the Humber keels to trade under sail, and he himself could remember sailing on her as a youth. Felton also had sailed. He had been in square-rig, and he had even been on a barge: 'Yes, I was up in London,' he had told me; 'Oh, it was some years ago now . . . I had the opportunity to make a trip—it was to Colchester—and so I went. . . . She was bigger than *J & M*. About 180 tons I think. . . . A coaster really. Very interesting trip.'

Now Felton sat tidily in an armchair in the saloon and said: 'You should've let me know that you were fitting-out, Nobby. I'd have been very glad to come along and give you a hand.'

Mollie said: 'It's the old trouble, Felton: we're short of money—as usual.'

He was horrified: 'I wouldn't have wanted *paying*.'

'Nevertheless it's easier to go it alone when things are tight,' I chipped in. 'You'd be the same.'

'Do you want any help now?' he asked.

Now I must admit that when opportunity knocks I am no sluggard. I had been more worried about the voyage south than I had cared to admit. *Weight*—that's what we lacked. And an additional male in the crew would be a godsend.

'How about Len here?' Felton asked when I had put the proposition of the voyage to him. 'What do you say, Len?'

'Oh, I can easily take a few days off work,' Len rumbled happily (he was a master tile-maker). 'I'd enjoy it. Have to ask the wife first, though.'

'How about your wife, Felton?' I asked.

'She won't mind,' he answered confidently.

I told them that it would take me at least four more days before *J & M* would be ready for sea. 'To be on the safe side, let's make the sailing date at tide time on the sixth day from now,' I said. 'That's May 1st.'

And so it was agreed. The arrangement was that Felton would let me know the next day if it was all right with both their wives; they would bring their own food supplies; they would pay for the train journey back to Barton-on-Humber where they both lived.

Mollie and I slept in peace that night, for the first time for many weeks.

But I had a faint nagging doubt as to whether I had done the right thing by introducing strangers into our lonely world.

7. FINAL PREPARATIONS

The next day showed that the delicate balance of our community had certainly been upset. We should have felt relieved with the promise of two extra male crew, but the strange calculations of our unconscious minds during peaceful sleep the night before had somehow arrived at the same conclusion: we did not want any intrusion into our privacy.

I tried to dismiss these thoughts as being unrealistic—dammit! additional crew would be an invaluable asset—but as I walked around the deck after breakfast I could not fail to note the evidence of their alien presence the day before: ropes cleated differently, the galley chimney not vertical, the mizzen stayfall not bowsed down neatly. . . . Nothing serious, but just irritatingly not how I would have done it.

Tigger prowled suspiciously, smelling daintily at every point of contact of alien flesh; Sym deck-walked and eyed the shore for strange intruders. Mollie? Well, she knew as well as I how such an offer out of the blue should be taken with gratitude, and yet there was a reluctance to accept their aid. Kester, lacking caution, said: 'I'll bet we could manage without them.'

'Well, perhaps they won't be able to come,' I said. 'Let's wait and see.'

Whatever the outcome, J & M had still to be finished in time to lock-out on 1 May.

First, the stayfall had to be unwound from the windlass and stored in the forepeak. I clamped two heavy wire grips on the fall between the stayfall blocks (I no longer used a rope stop—the bargeman's method—as it was awkward and time-consuming), lifted the pawls from the windlass, and left Kester

83

to get on with it. It was a fiddly job, but he could manage.

Before he fought the wire down through the small hawse-pipe in the deck, I broke out the mainsheet and blocks and dragged them aft. Then I let go the peaks and lowers (brails), and unwound the main brails a few turns before knocking off the winch handle with another handle so that the mainsail unfolded at a run. Another shower of dried grass, dirt, ochre and water fell to the deck; it is surprising how much muck can be concealed in the folds of a barge's sails!

It was a sunny morning, fortunately with only a slight breeze from the north, so the sail barely moved in the light airs. I shackled the mainsheet thimble to the clew, then the two patent-sheave single open metal blocks to the two cringles up the leech; I overhauled the mainsheet, hooked the large wooden mainsheet block to the heavy iron traveller ring which encircled the main-horse and hauled out the mainsail as far as it would go. I cleated the mainsheet to the bar which passes through the centre of this double-sheave block and extends about six inches on either side, and stepped ashore to examine the sail from a distance for any wrong leads or other flaws. It looked all right from the east bank. I jumped into the skiff, which we had towed behind us from Brigg, sculled across the river, and had a look from the west—the sunny side. She looked good from there. I sculled back, cast off the main-sheet and brailed up the mainsail, leaving the block hooked to the traveller—*not* a recognised bargeman's method, but a simple answer for a weak crew; bargemen unhook the block when the main is half-brailed to save overhauling too much mainsheet. But hooking-on and off in a blow can be a muscular struggle, so I had fitted a slightly longer mainsheet (3-inch, four-strand manila with a rope core), and always sailed with the hook of the mainsheet block moused to the traveller.

I was prepared to hoist the topmast next, when I suddenly remembered that we did not have a bob. Worse: we were out of bunting! To sail without guidance from the bob was un-thinkable. Had Mollie got any suitable material?

A prolonged search through every drawer and cupboard produced an old linen tablecloth which had been dyed dark blue over a printed pattern, and a remnant of white silk from her parachute-packing days in the Wrens.

'Make it into a swallow-tail,' I suggested. 'Use the tablecloth for the base, and the silk for the swallow-tail. Then I'll sew it to the swivel framework.'

Whilst she was making up this 2' 6" by 6' flag, I contacted the lock-keeper and tried to make arrangements to lock-out on 1 May. Tide time was around midday, and he expressed some doubt as to whether we would be able to get out.

'I have to give priority to the fuel barges,' he explained.

Now I had had quite a bit of trouble when I had tried to lock into the Ancholme five years before. *J & M*'s total beam, with leeboards, was only three inches less than the width of the lock, and unfortunately the sides of the lock tapered inwards towards the bottom. Consequently, the lock-keeper (the same one as now) would only take her through 'on the level'— i.e. when the tide outside was at the same level as the water inside. Locking-in was easier than locking out because then there had been virtually no risk of *J & M* dropping and jamming into the 'vee'; now it might become a risk, unless the lock-keeper could keep the locks quite free of traffic—and he couldn't guarantee this if he had to give preference to the fuel barges.

'I know most of them,' I told him. 'I'll have a word with whoever wants to go through.'

But I didn't feel very confident of success—not with those bash-on-regardless tanker skippers.

'Did you get the O.K.?' Mollie asked, looking up from her bob-sewing.

'No,' I said, and told her why. 'Every bloody step is a fight. Oh well—,' and I sighed deeply.

The bob looked fine. I sat down with palm and needle and round-seamed it through some stout tape to the metal framework. Then I climbed aloft with a length of codline and stood on the mast-cap whilst Kester made fast the bob and my

18-inch Stilson; I hove them up, screwed the staff into the topmast truck, and the job was done.

And it was time for lunch.

No sign of Felton. . . .

The gongoozlers had an interesting morning. . . .

By afternoon, the balmy breeze of the morning had backed into the south-west and increased in strength.

'We'll be able to hoist the topm'st,' I told Kester, 'but there's too much wind to bend the tops'l to the hoops. We can do it tomorrow morning before the wind gets up.'

Together we hoisted the topmast without any snags. We shackled on the rigging screws and set them up, set up the topmast backstays, set up the chain mainsail tack tackle, bent the topsail yard to the topsail halliard via a length of rope and hoisted the still-made-up-in-stops sail as far as the hounds. Then I climbed aloft and lashed the yarn to the starboard spreader, unfastened the rope span, and shackled the topsail halliard direct to the iron band around the centre of the 9-foot yard; part-way down the rigging, I shackled the topsail sheet to the clew, put a couple of temporary lashings around the sail and shrouds to prevent it from flogging, and finally shackled the tack to the wire which led to the tack tackle— on J & M this was set up to an eye-bolt on the spreet, with a separate cleat above the topsail sheet cleat, which was positioned as usual some two feet or so above the foot of the spar.

Lastly, Kester and I struggled the staysail forward of the windlass and hanked it to the topmast forestay. We shackled on the sheets (no tackle to control this powerful sail—only single sheets, and skilful rapid cleating when tacking), and made the sail up along the starboard foredeck with three stops. Bargemen generally harbour-stowed this sail aloft in a similar manner to the foresail, but I preferred to save the labour and keep it on deck. Besides, I could cover it up if it happened to rain. Lastly, Kester volunteered to sweep the decks whilst I hauled bucket after bucket of water to wash away all the dirt from the day's efforts.

Still no sign of Felton.

But that evening Owen Scrutton turned up.

I had worked as Owen's only surveyor on the pipe-line job for eighteen months, and he and I had slotted together in a perfect dovetail from our first union. As the contractor's agent, he was responsible for the business side of the whole project; as surveyor, I was responsible for the thousand and one snags which can crop up when routing a 21-inch water pipeline under nearly twelve miles of Lincolnshire soil. It had been an exhilarating experience for me, because I had never surveyed anything in my life—a point which naturally I neglected to tell the contractors when they employed me. To their question, 'Can you use a level?' I had replied: 'Of course'; I discovered later that they had been referring to a Dumpy and not a spirit level. Supply and demand are queer companions in adventure: the agent had demanded a surveyor, but urgent advertisements had failed to supply one. I was told about the job: I applied, I rejected automatically their first pay offer, a higher rate was agreed, I signed on. . . . Only then did I set to work to learn how to become a surveyor.

Owen, of course, had known a little about my ignorance: he had thought that I hadn't touched the trade since before the war and that I was a bit rusty. 'Where ignorance is bliss . . .' But Owen was a big man mentally as well as physically: he had employed me to do a job, and from the first day he had left me alone to get on with it. I did. We finished that contract ahead of schedule. The job was so successful that I was asked by the contractors to agree the quantity survey when it was completed. So for three months I became a quantity surveyor. The whole episode had been a most exciting adventure and I had thoroughly enjoyed it.

Now Owen had come to help me.

'I remember you telling me about the bad leak you had when you sailed here,' he said; 'so what about taking a three-inch sludge pump with you on the trip? I've got several for the contract I'm on at the moment, and you're welcome to borrow one if it'll help. You can shove it on a train once you get there, and bill the carriage to my contract. That'll save you any expense.'

When manna droppeth from heaven, it is wise to eat, and not to question the strange ways of the gods. The next morning, just after eight, a lorry from Owen dumped a two-wheeled motorised sludge pump on the wharf; Kester and I, using the double burton on the spreet, deposited it on the port quarter deck, from where the 3-inch hose could be lowered into the bilge well in the after cabin. Its presence was a marvellous comfort to me.

Still no sign of Felton. . . .

And not a breath of wind. . . .

'Let's bend the tops'l to the hoops,' I told Kester. 'You hoist whilst I tie.'

I cut six lengths of spunyarn and slipped them through my belt, and then lay aloft, releasing the ties around the top-sail and shrouds on the way up. I sat on the mast cap facing forward, the topsail halliard leading down behind my right shoulder to the headstick, and called to Kester, who had unfastened the halliard from the cleat on the port side of the mast: 'O.K., Kes. Haul away.'

He heaved his weight against the newly-rove 2-inch fall of the double/single topsail halliard tackle, and bit by bit the yard crept up until the first thimble in the luff was level with my face. 'Right!' I shouted.

I lashed the top hoop to the thimble.

'Up again!'

Slowly, lashing by lashing, I completed the six hoops— leaving the spare seventh resting free on the cap.

'Lower away—slowly!'

As Kester released the halliard, I fed the sail down to my right where it folded into an ungainly heap at the top of the shrouds. I climbed down the port rigging to avoid it.

'Right. Tops'l sheet, Kes,' I said, and did nothing to help as I wanted to see if he remembered the drill for hoisting the most important sail on board. He had not forgotten.

First to the centre cleat on the starboard shrouds—the topsail

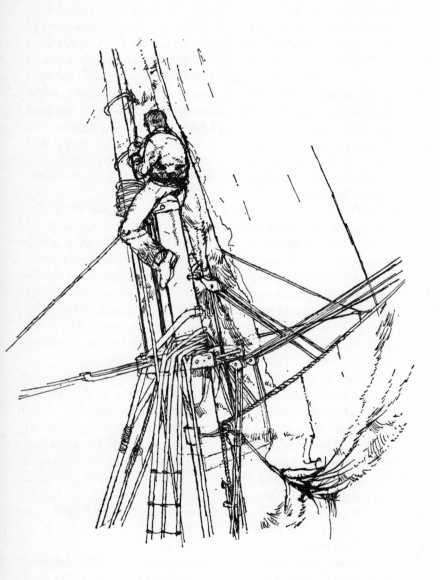

clewline: lift the coiled rope off the cleat, capsize it on deck, cast off the turns from the cleat. Then release the topsail tack tackle—on *J & M* the cleat above the sheet cleat on the spreet. Then down to the topsail sheet, turn and face forward (for the tackle is only a whip, with a fairlead block fastened to the stanliff for easy hauling) and haul away until the foot of the topsail is taut and the clew is tight to the block at the peak of the spreet. Finally, to the topsail halliards on the port side of the mast—a long, long haul is this one. Once the topsail is hoisted, bowse down on the tack tackle and make fast; then coil the fall of the clewline and cleat loosely; finally, coil the many fathoms of topsail halliard and sling it on the cleat. Topsail hoisted!

'Let's set the lot,' I said to Kester. 'You take the mizzen.'

First, he released the mizzen peak brail; this was fastened to the port forward mizzen shroud and acted as a wang when the sail was stowed. Then he released the throat brails cleated to the starboard side of the mizzen mast-case, and finally the boom topping lift, cleated immediately above. He ducked under the mizzen forestay, uncleated the mizzen sheet from the port side of the mast-case and overhauled the slack. The chain which held the sheet tackle to the rudder blade rose, dripping, from the water. The mizzen was set.

'Now the mains'l.'

Kester unhitched the sheet from the block hooked to the traveller on the main-horse, whilst I let go the inner and outer brails from the cleats on the after main shrouds, the middle and lower brails on each side of the mast case, lifted the pawl and unwound a few turns on the main brail winch and then banged the handle off as I had done before. As the mainsail unbrailed (and deposited another shower of muck on the deck!), Kester overhauled the mainsheet, and caught a turn around the horns of the block. The mainsail was set.

'Fores'l next.'

This was easy. Kester went to the foresail halliard, cleated to the port forward main shroud, to haul the tightly wrapped sail as high as it would go on the forestay. At least, he tried to do this, but his weight was insufficient for the task. As he unhitched the halliard from the cleat, both hands grasping the rope, the weight of the made-up sail which was already hoisted three-quarters up the forestay, was greater than his, in spite of the single-whip tackle; his feet left the deck as he began to rise into the air. With a quickness of mind which was remarkable, since he had not sailed on *J & M* for five years, he dropped his left hand, grabbed some slack rope and caught a turn on the cleat as he went past. Somewhat shaken, he made fast.

'Look,' I roared, and pointed to his feet.

When he had lifted the coils of halliard off the cleat he had capsized them correctly enough on the deck. But instead of capsizing them *away* from directly under the cleat, he had actually stood on the centre of the coil when he unhitched the halliard!

'If you ever do that again, Kes,' I warned him, 'I'll keep you shut up down below whenever we sail. If you'd let go of the halliard just now, the fores'l would've just run down to the foot of the forestay. But you, you twit, would've been hoisted by a leg up as far as the fairlead on the shroud and I suppose that by now we would be phoning for an ambulance to come and collect one dim-witted boy with, at the very least, one broken leg and one bashed-in head. Never, never, *never* stand on or in coils of rope which are being handled—you know that as well as I do. Now, come on, let's get this fores'l up.'

As we heaved in unison, it occurred to me that I would not be able to bawl at Sym for making this mistake. It was another mental worry to add to the growing list.

With the foresail hoisted, all I had to do was unwind the downhaul which had been coiled around the now-vertical sail (rather like a maypole), until just one turn remained; then I flicked this off, and the sail fell down the forestay with a swish. I spliced a length of new rope to the tack, bowsed down to the eyebolt in the stem-head, and the foresail was ready for sea.

I looked at the staysail. 'Shall we?' I asked Kester.

'Yes, come on,' he said eagerly.

The staysail halliard led to a cleat on the starboard forward main shroud. There was no tackle at all in this lengthy hoist—just straight up to the topmast hounds and down to the staysail peak, some twenty-five fathoms of 2-inch sisal.

'I'll hoist,' I said. 'You watch the sail for snagging.'

The power of a barge's staysail can be very frightening, mainly because there are no tackles to contain it. A single-part halliard, and two single-part sheets, to control a devil made of 12-ounce cotton duck, some sixty-six feet in the luff and ten feet across the gore, does not seem particularly sensible —or even adequate. It works, indeed it is an essential driving sail, in light airs up to about Force 4; above that is dicey, although trading barges anxious to save a tide might carry on if necessary. Needs must when the devil drives!

The strain on the topmast is fantastic. Shrouds and backstays will creak protest, and the spar itself will be twisted into an elongated 'S' by the combined stresses of topsail and staysail. Hanked as it is to the topmast forestay, it is not over-difficult to smother when lowering in a breeze, so the greatest dangers are the stresses which it imposes on the gear, and the handling of the sheets.

The method of sheet-handling is simple enough. When tacking (called 'winding' on a barge), the mate will put the foresail on a bowline—that is, he will pass a short length of rope which is attached to the upper cringle on the leech of the foresail twice around the forward main shroud and flick the end once over its standing part (if the staysail is not set, he will pass the end only once around the shroud and hang on to it). He will then crouch by the leeward staysail sheet cleat, (the position varies: on *J & M* these were at the forward end of the rigging chocks), and wait until the sheet begins to lift as the wind spills from the sail. Then he casts off the sheet, and nips across the deck to the opposite cleat. As the staysail flicks across the forestay, he must haul in and cleat immediately, because within seconds the wind will begin to fill the sail on the other tack, and it will be quite impossible to do anything

except catch and turn and hope that the sail doesn't flog itself
to pieces, or tear the topmast out, before another tack can be
made. The 'safety' period, I suppose, is about ten seconds.
The moment the sail fills, even in a light breeze, the sheet
is transformed from a length of flexible rope to a metal bar—
absolutely and uncontrollably rigid.

With the staysail hoisted, *J & M* looked complete and ready
for sea. Kester and I went ashore to admire our work, and even
Mollie broke off work in the galley for two minutes to stand
on the wharf and just look. The transformation from chaos to
order, from deck-strewn ugliness to 70-foot tall grandeur,
was a relief to the mind and a pleasure to see. Our new bob
fluttered gently, and *J & M* squeaked her warps as the five sails
caught the breeze.

'Come on, Kes,' I said. 'Let's stow 'em all now.'

Staysail first: Kester let go the halliard, whilst I gathered the
sail. Mainsail next: Kester let go the mainsheet, whilst I
cranked on the main brail winch; then I hauled the peaks,
and he made fast the lowers. Down foresail: Kester released
the halliard as I gathered the downhaul; I passed a couple of
turns around the closely gathered luff and continued to pass the
downhaul as Kester struggled to hoist it again; one-third up
was as much as he could manage, and I had to help him with the
rest. Topsail: I released the halliard whilst Kester hove at the
clewline; then I let go the sheet as he continued to haul
in.

'You stow the mizzen,' I told him, 'and I'll make fast the
tops'l to the shrouds.'

A length of rope, shackled to the yard tackle block half-way
between cap and hounds, is passed around the topsail and
starboard after main shroud—similar to harbour-stowing the
foresail—to prevent it from flogging. It was never an easy
job because the width of the folds at the hounds was more than
my arms could encircle; it was therefore necessary to flick the
tail of the rope around the back of the sail—difficult enough in
a sheltered harbour, but very awkward when anchored in a
seaway, wind against tide, with the barge rolling badly. On

several such occasions the jerk of the roll, alternatively slackening and tightening the shrouds, had very nearly flicked me off; I did not like the job at all. But, like everything else with her gear, it had to be done; the clewline, like a buntline on a square-rigger, could only partly tame the flogging canvas—and just like a square-rigger, I had to lay aloft in order to stow this sail.

J & M had looked her magnificent best with all sails set; now, sails stowed, with running and standing rigging all a-tauto, she waited impressively for the lock-gates to open so that she could float once more, high, upon salt water. I was glad that I had taken all the trouble to prepare her for this voyage; like Queen Victoria, she had reigned for sixty glorious years, but in just two days she would have to face another, perhaps her last, battle. It was as well that she looked her best.

Lunch time . . . still no sign of Felton.

Gongoozlers came, and went. . . . *J & M* was worth looking at now.

I had bought a couple of stone of whiting for making into black putty to stop those seams; now, at last, I had to get the filthy job done. In the quantity needed, two pairs of hands were a necessity: one pair to mix and work the mix into the seams, one pair to control the skiff.

I had Kester: I had two pairs of hands.

After lunch, I filled my pipe carefully and lit up—it would be my last smoke for several hours. I poured a stone of whiting on to a flat sheet of iron which Kester had found and cleaned, added tar and began to mix—with my hands. Kneading, adding tar and a little boiled linseed as required, I soon had a ball of black putty. With arms tarred half-way to elbows, I stepped into the skiff and Kester sculled round to the port bow. Hacking off the putty with a putty-knife, with Kester hanging on to the rail to keep the skiff alongside, I began forcing the mixture into the seams. Something like one thousand feet of seams had to be stopped: the chore took us all that day, all the next, and part of the last morning before locking-out. It had to be done and it was done, as neatly and carefully as both of us

could drive our weary limbs. It was a long, strenuous, monotonous and exhausting task, and for all of the hours which I
worked I wondered whether the putty would hold—or
whether it would be washed out by the first seas we met.

Neither *J & M*, nor crew, were covered by insurance.
This man-made security was a worry-dispelling luxury which
I tried to buy, but could not afford. So I had only what I had
put into my ship—and a 3-inch sludge pump. And a crew. . . .

Felton finally turned up, on the last night. His diesel lorry
rumbled to a halt alongside *J & M*, and Kester called down
through the propped-open companion-way: 'It's Felton.'

He was dressed in a light grey lounge suit, which made
Kester's announcement of his name, and his association with
the maroon 10-tonner outside, all the more incongruous. It
should have been a maroon Bentley at least.

'Sorry I haven't been able to get along before,' he told us,
'but I've been trying to clear up all the urgent jobs. Len will be
O.K. Are you ready to go tomorrow?' To my nod, he said:
'Right, then, we'll be here about ten.'

I nearly—very nearly—said: 'Look, Felton, we think we'll
be able to cope by ourselves. As a matter of fact we've talked
it over and we *prefer* to do the job in our own time, unaided.'
But I didn't. It is always so very difficult to refuse freely
offered help. Instead, I said: 'Well, thanks again, Felton. See
you tomorrow.'

After he had gone, Mollie said: 'You ought to have said no.'

It occurred to me then that the cards which the fates deal
out can seldom be altered. Like everything else connected with
this voyage, or with life itself, the chances are given and can be
taken—or refused. But the basic, predetermined direction
remains unaltered.

8. A SLOW START

An hour's work first thing in the morning of 1 May completed the black puttying of all the seams. I washed the tar off my hands, using neat Teepol, for the last time. Everything that could be done had been done. From beginning to end, the task had taken me—and Kester—fifty days.

Mollie had not been idle at South Ferriby. She had bought the last oddments of this and that to bring our stocks of food up-to-date. We could feed in comfort for ten days, exist for a month. All this had been achieved within our capital of £150: the books were balanced, £16 3s. 8d. was left. It was not much, but it was a credit—in more ways than one.

There was a tanker waiting to lock-in, and another waiting to lock-out. The lock-keeper was dubious.

'I'll take the incoming one as soon as she can float into the lock,' he said. 'But there won't be much time to pass the out-going tanker before the tide makes its mark. I'll have a word with the incoming skipper, and you see if you can hustle the other one. And you'd better find out if he'll pluck you clear—there's no wind.'

'He will,' I said. 'Fortunately he's the same skipper who towed us down from Brigg.'

Felton arrived on schedule with Len, but I had little time to spare for niceties. Half-an-hour before high water, and the incoming tanker was still lying to her anchor in the little bay outside the gates.

'What the hell's he playing about at?' I asked the lock-keeper.

'He said he had to do something with his engine.'

He bloody *would*, I thought.

Twenty-five minutes to go. Come on, come on, I gritted, and chatted sweet nothings to the lock-keeper.

'Ah! here they come,' he said at last.

They got their anchor leisurely and motored into the already-open lock. The gates thumped shut; the sluices were opened; the tanker nudged into the Ancholme. Ten minutes gone.

The skipper of the outgoing tanker had been primed by myself, and he—bless him!—was on the ball. As the other came in, he was more than ready to depart—in fact he very nearly clobbered the other's stern as it cleared the gates.

Whilst he locked through I gave Kester the tail of the dolly wire, and he sculled across to the far side of the entrance to the lock and made fast. Felton and Len took the dolly handles and began cranking, whilst I threw off our bow and stern lines and scrambled aboard. *J & M* canted from the wharf and crept slowly towards the lock.

The lock-keeper was raising the road bridge which passed directly over the lock; he paused in his efforts to shout: 'The tide's on its mark!'

A raucous chuff-chuff-chuff, reverberating to us through the chasm of the lock, indicated that the tanker was through. The inner gates were opened—just in time to allow *J & M* to keep moving.

I straightened the helm, peered over the port rail, and shouted to Kester to let go the dolly tail. He flicked the rope off the bollard, jumped into the skiff, and sculled rapidly under the port quarter; standing on the skiff's jumping platform, he grabbed the quarter-board and hauled himself on deck, painter in hand. He hove the skiff in and made fast.

J & M had lined up beautifully. As the high sides of the lock passed, Felton, Len, Kester and I pushed, two a side, to keep way on her. The mast and spreet slid through the main road and I looked up to a blur of faces on both sides, suddenly realising that our departure had caused long traffic queues; the inner gates were shutting, the open Humber was ahead, the tanker was manoeuvring astern towards us; 'Keep shoving,' I shouted to the others, and sprinted forward.

The mate threw a heaving line. I grabbed it, made it fast to our best towing warp, and waved O.K. He overhauled the line, humped the spliced loop of the warp over a stern bollard, and gave the thumbs up to his skipper in the wheelhouse. I hurriedly caught a turn under the windlass barrel, with the bight over the bitt-heads. The warp squeaked protest as it took the strain. We were under tow.

'Take the helm,' I said to Felton, and paused in my efforts long enough to wave thanks to the very helpful lock-keeper. The bridge was already nearly down. Talk about efficiency!

A bloody-sight more efficient than you are, I thought to myself as I remembered my duties. I climbed aloft and released the topsail tie; I should have done that before we left, but what with the puttying, and worrying about whether we could get out . . . I slid down quickly, released the clewline and hauled out the sheet.

'Up tops'l,' I said to Kester, and left him to it.

Our tug had taken the down-river channel around Read's Island; soon we would be out in the Humber proper. I knew that there a six-knot ebb would already be rushing seawards.

I set the mainsail in a hurry; Len overhauled the mainsheet. Before he had made fast, I had hoisted the foresail and released the encircling downhaul. The tug mate waved; I replied; the puffing of the exhaust stopped, the tow-line sagged into the water, the mate flung the loop off the bollard and I hauled in the warp as quickly as I could, sparing only a second to wave my thanks for the tow. The skipper replied briefly from the wheelhouse door, then he opened up his engine and in a very short time the noise of the chugging diesel died away. We were alone.

And with the solitude came a rush of responsibilities which are only apparent to those who captain large sailing ships in dangerous tides. Suddenly I realised consciously what I had known all the time: the sun was shining from a blue sky, and there wasn't a breath of wind! And we were racing down river sideways, out of control, in the grip of the six-knot current.

The Humber is a terrifying river to both power and sailing
craft alike. It is not really a river, because it does not have a
source: it is more like an estuary. It is surveyed daily by a rota
of special shallow-draught vessels, and channel and bank
changes are available to anybody who cares to phone the
Humber pilots. Unfortunately, new channels are scoured, and
fresh banks erected, within the space of one flood and/or one
ebb, and there are not enough survey vessels to keep tabs on
everything.

Large ocean-going ships proceed up to Goole, on the River
Ouse. Sometimes, even although they have a Humber pilot on
board, they go aground on a new bank. They seldom live.
I had seen a 3,000 tonner completely and utterly consumed by
the deadly moving sand and mud inside a fortnight. I had also
seen a Humber keel touch the bottom whilst athwart the tide,
*and immediately she had been rolled over by the pressure of the
tide-race, with the loss of both crew on board.*

The Humber scared me stiff!

Now I had to manœuvre in its treacherous waters in a
flat calm!

I tried the helm, but *J & M* was as dead as if she were
aground. It would be a waste of time to hoist the staysail—
even the bob hung its silk swallow-tails lifelessly.

'We'll have to drudge down,' I said to Felton. Fortunately
both he and Len knew what to do.

Hurriedly I bent a line to a fluke on the main bower anchor—
in case we fouled anything. Then I released some chain over the
windlass barrel, watching the slack between windlass and fairlead sheave for the first jerk which would show contact with the
bottom. It snatched when five fathoms were out. I let another
fathom go. Suddenly, *J & M* spun round until her bows
pointed directly into the racing ebb. I watched the shore—
yes, we were dragging. Good.

I went to the helm, leaving Felton to tend the chain and
Len to wind on the windlass when necessary. Because my
ship was now partially held into the current by the dragging
anchor, I had steerage on the rudder. All I had to do was face

aft, looking down-river, and steer as in a car: left wheel to turn left, right to turn right. If the bows suddenly fell off sideways, then Felton would know that the anchor was no longer ploughing the bottom and he would release a little more chain; if *J & M* stopped and failed to drag astern then Len would know that she had anchored herself and he would crank in some chain. The main risk was that the anchor would foul wreckage, or an old mooring, or some immovable object—in this case we could but try to capsize the anchor by hauling in on the trip-line attached to the fluke. We were lucky: the anchor dragged freely.

It was obvious that we were not going to cover thirty miles to the sea on this tide without any wind. Neither was I anxious to spend a night on the Humber riding to an anchor.

Felton said: 'There's an eddy just below the entrance to Barton Haven. The keels and sloops used to bring up there, so it must be a good spot. I'll show you the exact position when we get there.'

We drudged on.

Kester, helped by the others, brailed up the mainsail, and dropped the topsail and foresail. I edged *J & M* closer and closer inshore as Barton crept nearer. This first passage after five years consisted of a half-mile tow and a three and a half mile drudge—we didn't sail an inch!

'That's about it,' said Felton some time later, and I let go another five fathoms of chain with a run. *J & M* brought up with a jerk, and the tide bubbled around her bows with renewed energy.

'It doesn't seem any quieter here,' I remarked.

'It'll be all right when the tide drops a bit more,' he replied, and he seemed to be quite sure of his facts.

I was a stranger to this mooring. What could I say?

Mollie had made a salad lunch, and we sat down together as soon as the sails were properly stowed, and I had made absolutely sure that we were not dragging.

'Do you want to go tonight, or tomorrow?' Felton asked as we ate.

'Tomorrow,' I said promptly. 'I'm not going down this river under sail in the dark.' I was quite positive about that.

'Well, Len and I can sleep at home tonight,' Felton decided. 'If we get down here about nine in the morning, that'll give us plenty of time to get her ready before slack water.'

The trouble with having an amateur crew is that they do tend to take matters into their own hands—and yet what Felton said was sensible really. If they went home it would save some food. . . .

But there were the ebb and the flood tides to worry about overnight, and an anchor watch would be essential to make sure that *J & M* didn't catch a turn of her chain around the anchor and start to drag. Oh well, I'd have to do it all. Was there any point in having a crew, I asked myself yet again.

Mollie decided that there were still a few bits and pieces she needed for the galley; she could go ashore with Felton and Len: Kester could go too. No, not Sym—he would be too much of a handful ashore. Felton said they could leave the skiff in deep water just inside Barton Haven entrance where it wouldn't dry out.

They had to row the skiff with two pairs of oars to battle against the last of the ebb over the hundred yards or so of river before they pulled into the creek which led into the haven. Sym protested loudly as they went; he wanted to go too! When the skiff disappeared from sight behind the tall Maltings which overshadowed the eastern entrance of the tiny harbour, Sym whimpered unhappily and went below down the propped-open companion-way. I sat on the sliding hatch alongside the sheel, the sun hot overhead, and began to go over what we had done, and what we still had to do.

I was quite sure of one thing: I didn't like the presence of relative strangers on board. Just two hours of sailing—no, drudging—with Felton and Len on board had been enough for me. But why? They had both done what was required of them. When action had started they had heaved and pushed and shoved and pulled with effort and purpose, and they had done

all the right things whilst we were drudging. Was it just me
who was being bloody awkward?

Yes it was, I decided. I resented their presence because they
limited my freedom. Going back carefully over my thinking
from the moment I had discussed the possibilities of locking-
out that day, I realised that if they hadn't been expected I
would not have departed. Of course I wouldn't. Not in a
flat calm. Or would I have grabbed the opportunity of a tow
out by the tanker I knew and then anchored in sheltered waters
behind Read's Island? I had done that before locking-in five
years before; it would have been an obvious solution now.

Whatever I would have decided, I had allowed myself to be
organised into starting the voyage in adverse conditions. And
yet neither Felton nor Len had actually said or implied any
such thing. It was simply because they were there. I knew their
time was limited, and instinctively I attempted the difficult
in order to avoid wasting it. This must be the main basis of
my disliking their presence: they represented a hidden driving
force which could persuade me, unknowingly, to attempt
action without considering my own natural rhythm.

I thought further. If we had been alone, and I had in fact
started the voyage, would I have brought up here off Barton?
I knew that I wouldn't. Once started, I would have kept going;
it is not in my nature to stop.

I wished again that I could think up some excuse for getting
rid of my crew. I'd be better off without them. Mollie would
be happier, Kester certainly would; Sym would relax again.
And without them we could take our time and work, as we
had worked throughout eleven years, for the partnership.

I wished—but I could not act. I believed that Felton and
Len were genuinely looking forward to helping us with the
voyage and I did not have the heart to put them off.

The tide had fallen almost to slack water. I surveyed the
pool in which we had anchored and understood why keels
and sloops had used it in the past. The lead-line told me that
we still had just over a fathom under us; to the east, a mud-
bank stretched a grey-black greasy shoulder well into the

river; to the west, a low crumbling stony causeway dammed the current. The five-storey Maltings gave complete protection against all winds from south-east through to south-west.

As I reasoned away to myself in the sunlight, with the slow patterning of ideas which evolve and revolve in such conditions, it occurred to me that the tide would have turned before Mollie and Kester got back, and that they would have a job to row against the current. This mooring had its snags: a steep-to mud bank in front of the Maltings for one thing— if the wind blew from the north and we dragged, *J & M* would be in a perilous position. I decided that when the tide turned I would drudge two or three hundred yards upstream to the other side of the entrance to the Haven. Here the mud was flat, there were no buildings (and therefore no eddies) and altogether it seemed to me to be a safer place to anchor. Briefly, I wondered if I was being contrary; simultaneously I decided that I was acting in a seamanlike manner.

Slack water lasted for exactly one minute. I watched a sodden cardboard box drift alongside, slow, and stop. There was still no breeze. The water was glassy calm. Then the box began to drift again, back upstream. *J & M* swung offshore. Within ten minutes the flood tide was bubbling around her bows and her chain was bar-taut.

I had chosen the slack period to crank in a few fathoms of chain, and when the tide had covered the broken causeway, now off the stern, I tentatively tried a few more turns. The strain on the windlass was considerable. The old familiar icy warning of fear of the mighty power of nature stirred the hairs on the nape of my neck. The anchor broke its grip. We began to drag.

Within seconds the rudder crunched into the now-submerged causeway. Without hesitation *J & M* swung sideways, bow pointing towards the Maltings. The starboard chine slammed relentlessly beam-on into the concealed barrier. The sluicing flood, now a deadly enemy, boiled under the port side. *J & M* listed—over, over. . . . At forty-five degrees she stuck; perhaps the resistance of the causeway balanced the pressure of the tide

—who knows? Some saucepans crashed in the galley. Sym scrabbled on deck, barking furiously. I clawed along the port deck to get to the windlass. To do what? There was nothing I could do. From quiet contemplation to terrifying catastrophe in a matter of seconds—that's the sea, the cruel sea!

And then, unaided, *J & M* began to come upright. As the tide rose she levelled slowly. I cranked in all the chain, fearing that the anchor would foul the hidden causeway. Suddenly she was on the move, drifting silently upstream. The entrance to Barton Haven opened up—I had a brief glimpse of our blue skiff made fast to the Maltings wharf to the east, a keel high and dry on a golden sandbank to the west—and then we were past. I fleeted some chain. The anchor bit, dragged, bit; the chain jerked. I gave her some more. The anchor gripped. The sun still shone; there was still no breeze; the river was still glassy calm. And yet, through my own foolishness, I had nearly lost her.

It was a sobering lesson. Only afterwards did I remember the capsized keel and the disappearing 3,000-ton ship. Only afterwards did I sit down in the warm sun and shiver from shock. Sym came to lick in manly sympathy. Many months passed before I told Mollie and Kester of that particular adventure.

They came back at tea-time: Kester sculling, and Mollie seated on the centre thwart facing forward. As the skiff left the shelter of the Haven, the current swept it rapidly towards me and a jubilantly-barking Sym.

'Turn round,' I bawled to Kester. 'Face the tide!'

With a few deft jerks in the sculling oar he pointed the skiff downstream, and as she came alongside I caught the heavy painter with a boathook and made fast.

'Why did you shift the anchorage?' Kester wanted to know.

'Because I feel safer here,' I said; 'and in any case I doubt if you could've sculled back against the tide.' I didn't add that I also wanted to inspect the starboard chine for any damage after the frightening crunching it had suffered on the causeway, and that I had deliberately edged *J & M* further inshore over the flats so that she would dry out that night.

Once afloat, the dictates of tide and weather are the master control. As soon as *J & M* had swung to the ebb, and shown that she was not dragging, I went to bed—we went to bed. Because I was doubtful about my ability to wake on schedule after such a long hibernation from the sea, I set the alarm to wake me fifteen minutes before slack water. I needn't have bothered, I beat it by one minute—in time to switch it off. Mollie was still fast asleep when I slipped out of bed, dressed, dragged on thigh boots, and went on deck through the half-closed companion-way hatch.

It was very nearly dawn. I could see the sheen of the muttering mud and feel the damp cold of the salty air. There was no breeze. Instinctively I looked aloft where I could just distinguish the limp black bob against the lightening sky. Quietly I opened the fore-hatch, and pulled the fo'c's'le ladder on deck. I lowered it over the side amidships, and then fetched our emergency torch from the galley. Sym, meantime, had padded softly after me watching my every movement.

'Don't you dare bark,' I whispered as I went down the ladder. His cold wet nose nuzzled into my neck. He understood.

As I had suspected when I picked the anchorage, the mud was not soft. Starting at the bow, I inspected every inch of the starboard chine, sometimes kneeling in order to see better. There was not a mark on it! I checked the rudder, and the lower gudgeons (which had already been weakened from the pounding on the Gunfleet ten years ago), but once again, as far as I could see, nothing had suffered. I squelched down both sides, examining my black putty stopping, but all was in order. Finally I had a look at the anchor, shiny-bright in the light of the torch from yesterday's long drudge; it was not fouled. As I stood there in the cold half-light, looking back at the black spars against the lightening eastern skyline and marvelling at her ability to get herself out of tight corners (for I had done virtually nothing to help her), I realised that the tide had turned and already it was around my feet. By the time I had waded back to the ladder it had reached the first step.

Sym whimpered a quiet greeting. I pulled the ladder up after

me, slipped off my boots, went below, undressed, and slid gently back into bed. Mollie was still asleep. Within minutes so was I. The last thing I heard was Sym snuggling back into his basket.

I awoke in warm sunshine and listened for a tell-tale creak or rattle of rigging which would indicate the arrival of a breeze. All was still.

Nobody arrived at nine—although we were ready to sail. The sea-wall opposite our anchorage was deserted. Apart from a trail of smoke from the Maltings, from what we could see of Barton Haven it, too, was devoid of people and activity.

Indecision: what should I do? If nobody turned up by the turn of the tide should I go—and to hell with a crew? I pounded the deck in an anxiety of conflicting thoughts. The weather forecast had promised only light easterlies, and these were useless in both strength and direction. But I had flown Gauntlets in the Met Flight at Mildenhall before the war, and I knew that one could never rely on their prognostications; it was a standing joke there: 'Of course we're never right. We receive reports from you and from shipping all over the world, and we sit down and work out complicated charts of what we think the weather ought to be like. But we never get up from our desks and open the window. . . .' It was no use relying on their light-wind forecast; it might well be a fresh breeze offshore.

Len finally turned up just after ten and I sculled over to him. He was politely apologetic.

'Felton listened to the seven o'clock forecast and thought it would be a waste of time coming down,' he reported. 'So he's taken on a tile delivery job to London. There was no point in me hanging around, so I'm on the job today. Felton said he would be back on Friday afternoon'—he saw the beginning of an explosion from me and went on hastily—'but he said that if you thought the weather was O.K., then you go on and don't bother to wait for us. He said that he can see the topmast from his house, and if you were still here on Saturday we could come down about nine. What do you think about the weather, Nobby?' he concluded.

I was angry—and yet once again I could appreciate the logic. 'I don't know,' I told him. 'I'll see.'

I was tempted—very tempted—to go. Mollie left it to me; there was no need to consult Kester. 'Let's go,' he insisted. 'Come on, Nobby.'

To waste two more days—or go now. But I knew only too well how a deceptive sunny calm can make anybody brave enough to vote in favour of action. This period would soon pass; grey skies, gusty winds and stormy seas would alter all our opinions. Best to be safe. 'We'll wait,' I said. Kester was furious.

And so we waited.

9. A DISASTROUS START

With two more days to waste, we slipped automatically into the routine which living afloat for eleven years had evolved. Mollie pursued her multitudinous household chores, which kept the accommodation spick and span and our stomachs filled. Kester retired to whichever space was currently free from interference and played with his toys or his imagination—mostly the latter, for his collection of toys was minimal. I kept guard for them both, and for myself, by alerting my senses to the rhythm of the tides, the weather, and the everlasting movement about me. Time passes rapidly when there is so much to do. We were never bored.

Sym eyed the shore continually. He had not done a thing since we left Ferriby, and we began to worry. I was torn between keeping him on board until nature forced him to relieve himself, or taking him ashore for a final fling before the voyage started. Tigger, of course, in the manner of all cats, accepted the change without protest. He made his contribution in his tray with selective care as though it always had been done like that; he neither complained nor rejoiced at the new living, but continued to eat and sleep and live as contentedly as before. A cat on a boat is a perfect worry-neutraliser.

I took Sym ashore at low tide on the Thursday. He scrabbled out of my arms as I tried to help him down the ladder and belted across the mud to the shore with a frenzy which indicated his dislike of soiling our nice clean decks. He watered the seawall in profusion, and added considerably to the humus of the soil thereabouts. Afterwards, it took half-an-hour and six gallons of precious water to remove all the mud. A dog on a boat is very nearly a perfect worry-maker. And the food!—

already the sea-air had transformed him into a mobile dish-washer and refuse-disposer.

As before, we had very little to say to each other. What was there to talk about? We knew the problems and the hazards which faced us, and we understood all the computations which could bring victory or disastrous failure; we were sufficiently integrated to make idle conversation unnecessary —as useless as talking to one's self. We were tuned-in to an extent that often we knew what the other was thinking or wanting, so almost instinctively we moved on to the higher plane of trying to absorb the rhythm of nature about us. Only our portable radio kept us in touch with the other world which lay one hundred yards off our port or starboard beam depending on whether the tide was ebbing or flowing. That radio, when turned on, was the only false element on board.

The weather broke on Thursday night. Gusty squalls of rain woke me before my scheduled turn-of-tide awakening, and I had to get up to check. The wind was south-east, wet and cold. But it was from over the seawall and we were sheltered. I watched our position, we were not dragging; I went back to bed.

All day Friday was wet. Towards evening the rain slackened and the wind began to veer.

At the top of the tide it was round to the north-east—fresh; on Saturday morning it was the same.

J & M was snubbing irritably at her chain from the combined pressures of wind and tide when I sculled ashore to pick up Felton and Len at exactly nine. At least they weren't late! The grey clouds were low and thick and the wind was Force 5, rising 6. Going ashore was easy, coming back needed both pairs of oars. We scrambled aboard over the sheltered starboard side, and I looked up, for the hundredth time to the flicking bob. The weather forecast had said moderate northerly winds; here we had a fresh north-easterly. I brushed aside Felton's apology for missing Friday 'We couldn't have gone any rate in a sou'westerly,' I told him. We could, of course— at least as far as Grimsby; now we would have to beat to Hull before we could free our sheets—it was difficult to know exactly, with the dog-leg change of course.

'Are you going to wait for the tide to turn?' Felton asked.

'No damn' fear,' I said. 'There's ample wind to keep us turning over the tide. Let's get cracking now.'

I removed the prop from the half-open companion-way, after I had bundled Sym down below, and closed the hatch. In this brief moment the houseboat was again transformed into a ship of the sea.

'I'll take off the tops'l tie,' I told Felton. 'You and Len set the mains'l.'

As I climbed aloft the wind seemed to increase. Now that action was about to commence I tasted the same sicky fear in my mouth which I had suffered so often in the past, through war and peace, and wondered equally as often if others went through the same hideous process. As I flung off the turns of the topsail tie, I actually shivered with fear—not cold—as I thought about what I was attempting to do; like visiting the dentist, I discovered every possible reason why we should delay the departure. But I said nothing. I climbed down, released the clew-line and hauled out the topsail sheet.

By this time, the mainsail was set—slashing furiously against the harness of the sheet block which clanged and battered the traveller to and fro against the wooden main-horse.

'You go aft—and stay there,' I told Kester who was preparing to hoist the topsail. To his protests I said: 'There's too much wind about for you to handle the gear. Now you just stay aft of the main-horse or I'll have to send you down below.'

The topsail cracked boisterously as it went up. I made fast, and taking my time (to indicate nonchalance) I coiled the fall over the cleat. Then I bowsed down the tack.

'Right, Felton and Len, you start getting the anchor.'

Whilst they fitted handles and began cranking (the slowness of the tell-tale clanking of the pawls indicated that it was a hard grind), I hoisted the foresail to the top of the forestay and cast off all the turns of the downhaul except the last two; I hauled the sheet across the fore-horse and made the bowline

J & M immediately after purchase and before conversion

Left: J & M before conversion, the author a the helm. *Below:* J & M at New Bridge, Brigg. In this kind of weather she was snug and comfortable down below

fast to the starboard forward shroud. Then I lowered the port
leeboard about half-way.

I went forward and peered over the bow to judge the angle
of the bar-taut chain. It was about half-way in.

'Phew!' puffed Len.

'Come on,' I said. 'A bit more.'

I faced aft, with my right hand between his two on the
handle, and this livened their efforts.

'Clank,' went the pawls, 'clank . . . clank . . . clank, clank,
clank—'

I kept an eye on the angle of the chain, for it wouldn't do
to break out the anchor unintentionally on the wrong tack
this close to a semi-lee shore.

'Right, that'll do. Unship the handles.'

I went aft to the helm and gave her a sheer to port.

'Let go the fores'l,' I shouted to Felton.

He released the last two turns of the downhaul and the foresail bellied out, forcing the bows further to port. We were
turning.

'Get the anchor,' I bawled, and hurriedly centred the wheel
before adjusting the starboard wang, then the mainsheet. By
the time I got back to the helm she was well and truly under
way and beginning to swing into wind. Hastily, I corrected
the swing.

Felton waved his hand, after peering over the bow, to
indicate that the anchor was a-weigh. With a bone in her teeth,
J & M smashed across the short waves, heading slightly
upstream, towards the northern shore. This was the losing
tack.

The tide had about an hour and a half to flow, so we were
reasonably safe from most concealed banks with our half-
fathom draught, but our heading was towards North Ferriby,
where the channel is split by all sorts of hazards, and I decided
to stick reasonably closely to deep water.

'Ready about,' I shouted. 'Lee-O!'

I eased her to starboard, and then gave her full helm and
locked the wheel with the fid. I nipped across to the starboard

H B

capstan and lowered the leeboard about half-way; then across to the opposite capstan to crank up the port leeboard; then back to the helm in time to prevent her bows from sagging away to leeward.

'Let draw,' I shouted to Len. He released the bowline and the backed foresail whipped across the fore-horse—the chain sheet fetching up against the starboard rigging chock with a crash. 'Ease it across!' I bawled.

In spite of my fitness, I was panting after these exertions. I dropped the fid again and adjusted the port wang. Now we were all cleared for sailing.

This port tack was our best leg, with the bows very nearly pointing down-channel, although our leeway, plus the tide, was forcing us relentlessly across to the south shore. Still, it certainly wasn't a losing tack, because by the time we had to wind again we were a good half mile further downstream than when we started.

'Ready about. Lee-O!'

This time Felton cranked in the starboard leeboard as I lowered the port. It certainly made tacking easier!

'Let draw!'

Len eased the bowline round the shroud, and the foresail slid across the port without a crash, which can so easily rip the clew clean out of the sail in a strong wind.

'Do you have to crank in the weather leeboard at every tack?' Felton wanted to know.

'If you don't, it floats up alongside like a ruddy surfboard,' I explained, 'and that strains both the board and the tackle. Barge skippers don't generally bother—but then they don't have to buy new gear. I always hump it up unless there's not much wind. Better safe than sorry.'

'Shall we give her the stays'l?' Felton asked next.

'No, I don't think so; bit too much wind.'

Whether the wind had dropped slightly, or we had passed through a stronger area of contrary current, I don't know, but certainly we did not gain quite so much on the next making tack.

'I think she'd do better with the stays'l,' Felton said as we winded. 'Let's give it a try.'

I hesitated.

'I'll hoist it next time we tack,' Felton persisted. 'Len can leave the fores'l on the bowlin', and look after the sheet. We should be able to get it set whilst she's still head-to-wind.'

'Oh, all right,' I said reluctantly. 'But for heaven's sake get it right up and sheeted before we're round. I don't want it flogging for a whole tack.'

We reached the north shore.

'Ready about. Lee-O!'

By the time I had dropped the starboard leeboard and hoisted the port, and checked the swing on the helm, the two of them had set the staysail and sheeted it very nearly home.

'Let draw.'

The foresail slid across.

'You'll have to set the mizzen now,' I shouted to them as they stood back to admire their handiwork. *J & M* was tending to bear away under the pressure of that lofty staysail and she needed quite a lot of weather helm—too much!

They came aft and set the mizzen. Now she was happier.

There was no doubt that the staysail was a considerable help: *J & M* was pointing higher, and moving faster across the tide. I'll have to give her more leeboard on the next tack, I told myself as I looked aft and noted the wake creaming away off the port quarter at a greater angle than usual; I knew that the board could not be lowered further whilst she was leaning on it!

We made a much better gain on that tack.

'I thought the stays'l would help her,' Felton said smugly after we winded, but I was not happy about the strains imposed on the topmast and I told him so.

'Look at the shape,' I said.

The danger sign of the elongated 'S' shape could be seen quite clearly.

'I think we better have it off,' I said, but Felton remained obstinate. And like a greenhorn I allowed him to cajole me, with Len supporting his argument.

'If we reach Hull by slack water,' he pointed out, 'we'll have the tide with us all the way to the sea.'

It was a moot point. As soon as the tide turned we would be swept past Hull within minutes anyway. Foolishly, not wishing to offend my unpaid crew, I carried on against my better judgement. The fault was entirely mine, of course.

We winded again off the northern shore and on this tack I found that I could almost fetch New Holland Pier—used by the large Hull ferryboats. Now that I was getting the feel of her, I began to relax, although I still was not happy about the staysail. But I told myself that in six or eight more tacks we should be round the dog-leg, and then we could just about keep her on the port tack all the way to the sea—and the staysail could come off her directly we headed down that reach.

As we closed the New Holland Pier, the wind became fickle: it was blowing directly from Hull now, and the interference of the city was ruffling its smooth flow from the North Sea so that it came at us in chunks and flurries, with eddies swirling and swooping from different angles. I didn't risk going too close to the pier.

'Ready about. Lee-O!'

Len stood by the starboard staysail sheet, and Felton was at the bowline. Kester was still aft, sitting on the port side of the coachroof with his feet on the sludge pump. Mollie, Sym and Tigger were below. I bore away slightly, and then gave her a few spokes to commence the roundup into wind. I heard a single grunt of expiring power and felt an immediately life-lessness in my ship; simultaneously I looked aloft just in time to witness the graceful movement of the broken topmast as the top two-thirds arched to starboard from the drive of the topsail and staysail, and crashed, inverted, into the starboard shrouds.

We were still winding. Without knowing what I was doing I continued to crank on full helm. The drive from the topsail

and staysail had gone, but she carried way. Instinctively I
fidded the wheel and dropped the port leeboard; in a trance,
I wound up the starboard leeboard. Automatically my mind
cash-registered our depleted funds: 'Less than £16,' it told
me, 'less than £16.' I stared glassy-eyed into the future.

Then: 'Let draw!' I shouted, and as an afterthought:
'Are you O.K. up forward?'

Len had flung himself to port across the front of the mast;
Felton had dived behind the mast. Neither had been touched by
falling debris. My thoughts skipped briefly and thankfully over
the news that they were unharmed: uninsured, Passenger
Risks, Common Law, claims—well, *they* were O.K.—claims,
new topmast, under £16 in the kitty, no insurance, how to
survive? What to do? Where to go? Shock-blindness: a
confusion of thoughts hustling for a decision. Mollie through
the after hatch: 'What's happened?' Sym barking hysterically
down below. Len struggling to get the staysail on board.
Where was the topsail? Felton asking: 'Shall I lash the broken
bit to the rigging in case it slips?' Computations: three and a
half miles back to Barton Haven; tide with us; barge handling
quite nicely on a reach; should be there in half an hour. Put into
Barton? How to get in under sail? Fair wind, but no topsail:
she'd go dead on me under the lee of the Maltings.

Len: 'Felton, give me a hand with this stays'l.'

Mollie: 'What are you going to do?'

Kester: 'Is this the end, Nobby?'

No, I thought, no—not the end. But less than £16. Where
could I get a lofty topmast on these dismal shores: 42-feet
overall, eight inches diameter at the base, five inches at the
hounds. Where? And the cost? I'd have to lower away again;
was the topsail torn? And the topsail hoops—had they gone
overboard? Where *was* the bloody topsail?

Len and Felton had dragged the sodden staysail on board—
staysail, sheets, halliard, wire rigging—a tangle of chaos. Both
of them were wet from the struggle. The topsail? It was still
aloft—half of it attached to the topmast stump (I counted three
hoops), the rest draping down the starboard shrouds (yes,

there were the other three hoops!). Even the bob was intact. I looked astern. The skiff was towing behind like a faithful dog; and there was no sign of floating wreckage.

And then the sun broke through. . . . It helped. The grey clouds were breaking up; *J & M's* red decks reflected warmth and comfort.

'The stays'l seems to be O.K.,' Felton reported; 'it's just in a bit of a taffle. As far as we can see nothing's been lost and nothing's torn or broken—apart from the topm'st. What happened?'

I said I didn't know.

Five minutes later he discovered the fault.

The port topmast backstay fall had parted—one of the two ropes on board which I had thought were unnecessary to renew! It had parted exactly where it passed over the sheave of the upper block. Like a fool, I had inspected both falls but I had not unrove them; I had forgotten this one position where wind and weather could attack and yet the result could not be seen visually. In spite of all my care, and the weeks of labour to ensure that *J & M* was as perfect as I could make her, nature had found a flaw in my work. I could not whine; it was entirely my fault.

Surprisingly, now that I knew exactly what had happened and whom to blame, I felt better. I'd made a mistake. Very well, I'd set to and put it right—somehow. Then we'd try again. But next time, I thought, next time we'll go alone. No more strangers. Just us—and *J & M.*

We dropped the anchor in exactly the same place that we had left nearly two hours before. Len and Felton were anxious to get ashore. They helped to stow the mainsail and foresail whilst Kester stowed the mizzen, but they refused Mollie's offer to stay to lunch.

The wind had slowly died away with the clearing of the sky, so that now it was no more than a fresh breeze. I landed Felton and Len just inside the Haven—on the steep-to mound of sand and shingle which I had noted when I had drudged past on Wednesday.

'I'll keep in touch,' Felton said, and with that he and Len pushed off.

The tide had made its mark. Already the bank on which I had landed, which very nearly blocked the entrance to the Haven, was showing six inches of wet sand. Disconsolately I climbed to the top, where the solitary Humber keel was perched like a monument, and looked down for the first time into the little port.

To the east, on the opposite bank, the Maltings towered over the narrow entrance. I could see now that what had appeared from the outside to be nothing more than a narrow creek, was, in fact, a snug pool of a harbour which was completely hidden behind the great hill of sand and shingle on which I stood—twelve feet high at least at low water. This extraordinary mound was so steep-to on the Maltings side that it was possible to dive into the creek from its shore at half-flood. Inside the Haven were half a dozen yachts, a clutter of small boats, and another keel. A youngish fellow was pottering on its deck.

I walked across the flat top of the sand-bank and down the gentle slope on the far side. The keel was moored fore and aft some thirty feet from the shore. It was a very small Haven.

'Good-morning,' I hailed; the young chap looked up. 'I've just lost my topm'st off New Holland Pier,' I explained. 'I'm skipper of the sailing barge outside. I'll have to get her in here to re-rig her. Is there a motorboat that could tow me in?'

His reply was more than a surprise.

'I've been watching you,' he said. 'You shouldn't have carried that stays'l in this morning's wind.' (Don't rub it in, I thought.) 'There's nothing here powerful enough to fetch you in against the current, so I thought I'd come down in case you wanted help. I'll be out there inside ten minutes—but we'll have to hurry or we'll miss the tide.'

'Thanks a lot,' I called; and then: 'How much for the pluck in?'

'Oh, forget about *that*,' he said, almost scornfully. 'I'm only too happy to help a sailorman.'

Suddenly it seemed to me that the sunlight glowed more brightly in tiny Barton Haven.

I sculled back to *J & M* with the glad news for Mollie and Kester. Hastily I cranked the anchor up-and-down, with Kester helping, watching the entrance for the first appearance of the keel. She slid out, circled, and came alongside from astern; the young skipper was still alone.

'Give us your line,' he said unhurriedly as he came out of the wheelhouse door. He took it from me and dropped the loop over his stern bollard. 'There's no room to manœuvre in there,' he went on, 'and in any case the tide's dropping fast. I'll circle off-shore and then head for the entrance. You keep to the Maltings side, and just before we reach the sandbank I'll throw off the tow. Keep her going straight in alongside the Maltings and you'll fetch up on a mud-bank. It's the only spot that's free, and she'll lie there nicely.'

'Couldn't we go in side by side,' I asked. I didn't like the idea of plunging blindly into a cul-de-sac.

'No room for that in the channel,' he said, and then, as he saw Mollie; ' 'Mornin', missus. Bit o' bad luck. We'll soon have you in a snug berth.'

He went back into his wheelhouse and nudged ahead.

Kester and I soon got the anchor, and I ran back to the wheel, telling Mollie to give Kester a hand to haul in the towing warp when it was released. The keel headed offshore, then circled to starboard and began the fast run for the Haven entrance with its diesel chugging loudly as the throttle was fully opened. Just before we reached the Maltings, he sheered to starboard and throttled back; he came out of the wheelhouse, lifted the tow from the bollard and held it whilst Mollie and Kester overhauled as much slack as they could. Then he sent the loop curling through the air to land on our starboard deck with a thud. A few seconds later I heard his diesel chug furiously as he went astern.

Silently *J & M* slid between the Maltings and the golden sandbank. The Haven opened up. Dead ahead, on the far side of the tiny pool, the creek headed straight inland. There was no sign of the mud-bank which was supposed to stop us, and less than fifty yards under our bows the clutter of rowing and sailing dinghies blocked the creek. All I could do was obey orders.

And then, quite silently, *J & M* slid to a halt. Concealed just beneath the very murky water was a mud-bank which fetched us up as if we were fitted with disc-brakes. Just six feet off our port beam was a stone wall with a gently sloping stone top which extended some twelve feet to one of the yellow brick Maltings buildings. Alongside our stern, the road into the Maltings turned down-stream at right-angles, and was protected from flood tides by a five foot stone wall. Our slightly-sloping 12-foot deep section was triangular in shape, about the same length as the barge, with its base to the road. Here the stone wall was only two foot six high at its lowest on our side and, of course, five feet from the road side. It was a wonderfully sheltered position.

On the opposite side of the Haven was a small boat-yard— quiet now, for it had gone midday, and it was a Saturday. But they had a wooden keel on blocks, presumably for repairs, and another alongside their sheds being converted; there were two half-built motor cruisers and an almost complete sailing yacht of about thirty feet L.O.A. in the stocks. The idea crossed my mind that I might be able to get a temporary job there.

Kester and I dragged warps fore and aft and I bound *J & M* into her new berth. We took our time—she was hard and fast on the mud bank and couldn't move. Our heavy gangplank spanned the gap easily.

A great peace descended upon us after lunch. An Ordnance Survey map, and our own eyes, told us that the Haven was very nearly a mile from the town of Barton-upon-Humber. The only buildings here were the Maltings on our side of the creek, and the boat yard and a few old workers' cottages on the other. Nobody seemed alive here. As the tide left us, the filthy mud was so soft that we half-floated in it, and the only sound we could hear was its constant muttering at our intrusion. There was no wind—the Maltings were a complete protection from east to north. The sun beat down into our sheltered corner and reflected off the bricks of the tall buildings, and the temperature rose . . . and so did the smell. . . . We learned later that all the sewage from the town came to the sea past *J & M*! There is no such place as a perfect berth.

But certainly we couldn't grumble. We were safe and snug, thanks to the un-named skipper (who had re-moored his keel, and disappeared for ever as far as we were concerned, before I had even poked our gangplank ashore), and in contact again with civilisation there was a good chance that I would be able to find a job, some money, and a new topmast—in that order. We still had plenty of food, there was nearly £16 left in the kitty, both Sym and Tigger could go ashore easily when they felt like it, Mollie could go shopping without difficulty (I would have to put some steps by the road wall), and if necessary Kester could go to school ('I don't want to,' he protested loudly). I doubted very much whether there would be any harbour fees, and I felt sure that I would be able to obtain water from the Maltings.

And so a good lunch, some warm sunshine, peaceful un-interrupted surroundings, and a careful counting of blessings, and I was feeling ready to face up to my responsibilities once again. The almost overwhelming shock which the loss of the topmast had given me was already far, far away in the past.

'Come on, Kes,' I said. 'Let's get the stays'l ashore and sorted out, and then we'll have a go at getting the tops'l and topm'st down without lowering the gear. It shouldn't be too difficult.'

It wasn't. By Sunday evening the job was done and *J & M* was bald-headed; ashore, on our private sloping wharf, were neatly stacked an undamaged staysail and foresail, and every last bit of rigging. Nothing had been lost, except the topmast—and we had both sections of that too.

10. TRY THE LABOUR

Appreciation of paradise is probably always directly proportional to the physical and mental anguish suffered on the way towards it. I thought—we thought—that Barton Haven was a little bit of paradise after the mostly-negative worries of the past few days, and there was some proof to indicate that our senses had not misled us.

For the low-water smell was a once-only affair. Presumably our noses made some necessary adjustments, because never again did we suffer the appalling stench which must have continued to rise from that odious slime. It is true that we could still *see* the basic cause when they opened the sluice a mile upstream at half-ebb, but the novelty soon wore off; after that we might just as well have been moored in a coral lagoon filled with sharks—we could not swim in the lagoon, so we ignored it.

Otherwise there were many clues to indicate that we had found a tiny paradise. Our benefactor of Saturday morning had silently departed, but he must have spread some news of our misfortune. How else could we explain the pile of Sunday newspapers which we found on our doorstep next morning? (I had re-erected the front door assembly on Saturday—a certain indication that I knew we were there for quite a time.) A note explained: 'Didn't know which one you took so left the lot.' It was not from a keen newsagent, and the fairies could not have dwelt anywhere near that smell—so they must have come from a local inhabitant.

We found out later that they had: from the father-in-law of the young keel skipper.

Then there were the vegetables which mysteriously appeared

on our port quarter overnight on many occasions—obviously dropped on to the deck from over the high wall which pro- tected the road. We never did discover who was responsible for all the deliveries, although Felton and Len were connected with some of them.

Schooling for Kester was arranged with surprising ease. There was a small village school half-way to the town on the opposite bank, and Mollie took him there on the Monday. The head mistress knew all about J & M, and welcomed Kester rather as if he were the sole survivor of a mid-Atlantic shipping disaster. If tide time coincided with his going-to and coming- from school, he would scull the skiff over the creek and leave it there; this was for convenience, not to create an impression, because otherwise he had a three-quarters of a mile walk up our bank to the first bridge with a quarter of a mile back on the opposite bank, and a repeat in reverse after school was over. I would not say that he enjoyed going, but the novelty of his situation certainly helped.

I soon found out that Barton Haven and Barton-upon- Humber had taken the misfortunes of J & M very much to heart. How much was Felton's, or Len's, or the young keel skipper's doing I never discovered, but it seemed that every- body in the area knew, and were prepared to help. Perhaps not quite everybody—there had to be a serpent, or it would not have been paradise—but certainly more people helped us than we had known before, and amazingly, they seemed to know instinctively what was needed.

There were the tow, the papers, the vegetables, and Kester's schooling. There were the men in the boat yard: 'If you want any help just let us know and we'll come round in the evening. Don't lay anything on during the day or it'll cost money'; the manager of the rope-walk which lay alongside the creek half- way into town: 'If you want any rope or wire just let me know; always pleased to help a sailorman'; the manager of the Maltings: 'Certainly you can help yourself to water; tell you what, if you need any fuel, take it from the bunkers. Don't whip the large lumps of anthracite though, that's what we use, but you can take as much as you like of the small stuff and the dust'; the skipper of the market-boat *Khama*, an ex-Humber sloop, which three times weekly collected produce to sell in Hull: 'When you're ready for sea just let me know and I'll give you a pluck out.'

There were the numerous shopkeepers who never failed to reduce their prices, using as an excuse: 'We always used to give a discount to trading vessels, so why not to you?' Either their arithmetic was poor, or they were grossly overcharging their public—or nostalgia was more important to them than business acumen. Whatever their reason they were mostly more than generous to *J & M*.

To *J & M*, be it noted—not necessarily to us. That we were a part of our vessel was an accepted fact, but I cannot believe that any of our voluntary benefactors were swayed by our financial problems—in fact, I cannot see how the majority of them could possibly *know* how little we had. The truth was that a sailing ship, an ex-trader, had put into their port in distress and they genuinely wanted to do their bit to help. Nothing was forced on us. It was all done very quietly and surreptitiously. We were the strangers in paradise.

Len faded out of our lives forever during the first week of our stay. He and his wife invited us once to tea (a North Country high tea), and we gathered from the general trend of the conversation that his wife did not approve of his gallivanting off to sea in strange ships. I tried to make the point that it had not been my idea, but I was wasting my time.

Felton, on the other hand, was determined to put us on the right road, although we had an idea that his wife, too, did not entirely approve of his coming with us—a point which we did not clarify until a couple of days before we left. In the meantime I was glad to receive his help, for he certainly seemed to have plenty of contacts.

He was not the only one who tried to find me a job. Whenever I met anyone, I introduced the subject into the conversation on the grounds that 'those who don't ask, never receive'. But Barton in this respect was very nearly a distressed area.

Nobody could offer either a job or a suggestion—except: 'Try the Labour.'

Before I started my quest to escape from the rut, whilst I was still in limbo between the worlds of what-I-should-be-doing and what-I-wanted-to-do, I had approached the Labour Exchange to see what they could offer. 'I see you've been flying in the RAF,' said the man behind the counter. 'Well, I've got just the job for you. They're constructing a new aerodrome at such-and-such and they want plenty of men to build the runways. How about that?' As a result of this and later experiences (although I had never used them again after that first effort), I knew that Labour Exchanges were only capable of exchanging labour: known to them as skilled, semi-skilled or unskilled. They were completely and utterly lost if called upon to extend their thinking beyond these simple terms of reference. But here at Barton, approaching insolvency, desperate measures were needed. So I took the bus to a nearby town and tried the Labour.

I suppose it is unwise to bounce into a funeral parlour and expect a cheerful reception. The dreariness of the surroundings had seeped into the very souls of the inhabitants as they battled grimly and continually with the misfortunes of others. A fug of menial corruption permeated the tawdry atmosphere; the ply and plastic decor was singularly appropriate. 'Yes?' queried a gnome from his burrow, and I put my problem to him as succinctly as possible. 'Wotsyertrade?' he snapped. 'Wotsorterworkjerwant?' I continued to beam cheerfully at him as I felt in my pocket and produced a sheet of paper which had taken me an hour to compose that morning. When one is forced through circumstances to approach government servants for help, it is as well to go prepared with an adequate weapon which will guarantee more than a standard bureacratic response. I unfolded the sheet, spread it on the counter, and pushed it over to him. He grunted, and began to read:

S/ldr D. H. Clarke, DFC, AFC (Ret.)

Born: 7.6.19   married: 16.2.42   one son, born: 12.11.46

List of Trades and Paid Employments since July, 1935

Prop-boy	Journalist	Designer
Compositor	Barman	Boat salesman
Bookbinder	House-painter	Wire splicer
Stone litho		
processor	Yacht painter	Commercial pilot
Machine-minder	Yacht deliveries	Insurance salesman
Commercial artist	Sailing Instructor	Sign painter
Foundryman	Barge skipper	Hedging and
		ditching
Block maker	Wild fowling	Hire-boat operator
Linotype operator	Sailmaker	Boat repairs
Monotype operator	Sail repairer	Weighbridgeman
Warehouseman	Yacht rigger	Road sweeper
Book-keeper	Fruit picker	Lorry driver
Store-keeper	Agricultural worker	Boys' club leader
Driver	Stack-cover repairer	Surveyor
Printing salesman	Barge rigger	Metal diviner
Fighter pilot	Shipwright	Quantity surveyor
Bomber pilot	Sparmaker	Laboratory assistant
Coastal command		Time and motion
pilot	Saw-pit	study
Ferry pilot	Caulker	Aggregates salesman
Transport pilot	Blacksmith	Backacter driver
Flying instructor	Glazier	Beet hoer
Test pilot	Electrician	Drag-line driver
Stunt pilot	Plumber	Inventor
Chief Flying		Fire extinguisher
Instructor	Author	salesman
Chief Instructor	Yard foreman	Commercial rigger
Explorer	Yard manager	Coalman

I watched his eyes scan this epistle as his brain tried to formu-
late a reaction. His semi-skilled training was inadequate to the
exigency: 'Just a minute,' he muttered, and shoved off. He

Unbending the sails. The author, Mollie, and Kester who was six at the time

Left: J & M at Mistley immediately after re-rigging the new topmast. *Below:* Mollie and Kester feeding the swans at Mistley. Sym looks on

reappeared quite a few minutes later in company with the manager. 'Please come into my office,' he invited.

Alas, as I expected, it was all a waste of time. No jobs were forthcoming nearer than Scunthorpe, and I could have found something there, via Owen Scrutton, without the assistance of the Labour. They were sympathetic about my distress, but the circumstances were beyond their powers. I must say that I went back to J & M with a sigh of relief; now I had to rely entirely on my own resources, but I had at least eliminated the possibility of naggers who might have cried afterwards: 'But you should have gone down to the Labour Exchange. That's what they're for.'

Felton, on the other hand, did a great deal to help. He came on board that first Monday evening with a bottle of wine and some hopeful encouragement. I must admit that I had been brewing nasty thoughts about him since we lost the topmast. I was in no doubt that the actual breakage was entirely my fault, because I had not checked those backstay falls thoroughly enough, but I could not help thinking that probably nothing would have happened if he had not pressured me into setting the staysail. We had enjoyed his company before we sailed, and now that we were back in port I was glad to see him again. I concluded that this was a typical case of incompatibility between ship, skipper and crew—which occurs more often than is generally supposed. But only after a vessel has left port.

'Have you been down to the Labour?' was very nearly his first question, and I told him what had happened. 'Yes,' he said when I had finished, 'I didn't think you would have much luck there.'

J & M's saloon had seen some conferences over eleven years. That evening of 6 May was possibly the most desperate. The Aladdin lamp gave a brilliant circle of light around the table, but the far corners of the room were filled with dark shadow. Mollie sat on the settee, knitting, and Felton and I lounged back in armchairs on the other side of the keelson. We had lit the Esse-Dura earlier, for the nights were still very cold, and the flames which flickered warmly through the glass doors reflected on the deck head of the inglenook. *J & M*'s saloon was a very comforting place to be in.

'I shall have to find a job of some sort,' I told Felton. 'I've less than £16 left, and that won't even buy a new stick for a topm'st. And we'll have to have some money for food. If I get a job in Scunthorpe, there's all the travelling to and fro which won't give me a chance to re-rig her. That's out—we'll be stuck here far too long.'

'Well, I can help you a bit there,' Felton said encouragingly. 'I know a timber yard in Hull who often import Oslo firs for scaffolding and ladders; we may be able to find one that's long enough. Also, I've got a load of bricks to deliver there on Thursday. If you'd like to meet me at the bridge at the top of the creek at seven I'll pick you up on the way to collect the load. You won't mind giving me a hand will you? I'll pay you the usual rate.'

'Of course I won't mind,' I told him. And so it was fixed.

The trip was a success. We loaded the bricks, and delivered them, in record time, and then drove to the timber yard where Felton was known. An individual of incredible proportions listened to Felton's explanation, and my requirements, in good humour and rumbled mirth into his reply: 'Just as well you came today,' he told us. 'There's nobody about, and we've just taken in a new shipment. But it's not going to be easy to find a pole that thick.'

'How much will it cost?' I asked anxiously.

'Oh, they're all the same price. Two and nine per foot run. But you're going to have to buy over a fifty footer to get the thickness you want. Now let me see,' and he fished thoughtfully through his mental files, 'there aren't many . . .'

He led us through the valleys between the piles of timber. He read the hieroglyphics at the foot of this and that, but continued to wallow, muttering, on his way. At last he stopped. He indicated just one pole, two-thirds from the top of a 10-foot high stack. 'That's it,' he said. 'Help yourself.' I looked at that heap of hundreds of firs and not unnaturally asked, 'How?'

He wheezed a chuckle. 'Like this,' he said. He seized the foot
of the fir and lifted and wriggled, and wriggled and lifted,
until suddenly it began to slide out; then he left it to Felton and
myself. 'If it's too long,' he wheezed breathlessly, 'there's a
crosscut over there. If it's not man enough, well it's the biggest
there is in the yard.' And he left us to get on with it.

That tree was fifty-three feet long, nearly nine inches at the
exactly circular base and three inches across at the top; at forty-
two feet it was a fraction over four inches diameter—it needed
to be about six inches to allow for stripping the bark and
shaping.

'It's too thin,' I told Felton, 'but if that's the largest he has
then I'd better take it.'

I borrowed the crosscut, trimmed my new topmast to forty-
two feet, and stowed the 11-foot offcut back in the pile. We
carried the tree to the lorry which was parked by our fat friend's
office.

'Find what you want?' he asked. Without further ado, he ran
his rule along the tree as we held it (I doubt if he could have
bent down). 'That's exactly forty-two feet,' he rumbled. He
consulted a ready reckoner: 'Five pound fifteen and six.' I paid
him with grateful thanks. 'That's all right,' he grunted. 'Always
glad to help a friend of Felton's. I'll keep an eye open for your
barge when you sail, just to see what the new mast looks like.'

'I'll come in close to this bank,' I promised him. 'But it won't
be for a week or two yet.'

During the long drive back to Barton, via Goole, Felton
started the talking. It had been a good day in all respects. We
had, according to him, loaded his lorry in record time ('You
certainly put your back into a job, Nobby; I've never had a
mate sling bricks so fast'), and the unloading had been a revela-
tion ('I've never seen a mob on a site so keen to unload quickly
What did you say to them?'). And he was even more surprised
at getting a cheque out of the Agent on the site ('Don't forget I
used to be in this racket,' I had told him. 'Get your money on
delivery; don't let it pile up').

On my part, I thanked him again for his help in getting the

topmast, but he seemed to think that I had done much more than he had.

'Why don't you come in with me,' he said seriously. 'You seem to know a lot more about the business side than I do, and you've certainly proved that you can work hard.'

For a moment I was tempted—but not for long.

'No, thanks,' I said. 'It's very nice of you to offer, Felton, but somehow it doesn't fit into my scheme of things.'

'But what do you want to do?' he asked.

The roar of the diesel in the cab relaxed my mind from the worries of the past few weeks, and the winding road unrolled an endless change of scenery as we sped towards the late afternoon sun over Goole. I was warm, comfortable, happy, and unworried. This was one of those brief moments of contentment which makes living outside the rut so attractive and worthwhile. I thought of the list I had prepared for the Labour Exchange. What *did* I want to do? I chuckled to myself as I told Felton in all seriousness: 'I haven't a clue.'

He looked across at me and said: 'You know, Nobby, I envy you your life. It's exactly what I'd like to do if I wasn't married, and I didn't have kids to bring up, and I didn't have a house and a lorry to pay for. How did you dream up the idea in the first place?'

'From books,' I said simply, and it was the truth. 'Before I joined the RAF in 1937, I had to commute daily to London from Westcliff. I loathed the train journey as much as I hated London, so I used to read escapist books of adventure to pass the time. Then one day I said to myself Why read? Why not get out of the rut once and for all—now? So I did. That happened one morning going up to Town; when the train pulled in I got out and caught the next one home. Then I joined the RAF. After the war—well, I just kept out of the rut.'

'But what about money?'

'Money is never as much of a problem as rut-dwellers seem to think,' I told him. 'This isn't the first time I've been caught out, and it won't be the last. I must admit though, that when it happens it's a worry—and I'm a first-class worrier. . . .'

'I don't believe it,' Felton chipped in.

'Thanks,' I said cynically; 'but I am. I doubt if anybody could be that thick-skinned. Being without money is a hell of a strain, believe me! But it's not the end of the world. We've survived eleven years of this sort of living and I wouldn't swop it for anything.'

'But Mollie never seems to worry either.'

'Don't you believe it,' I told him. 'We both worry like hell when we're out of money, and Mollie does more than I do. One day,' I added thoughtfully, 'we'll have to stop it and settle down. Perhaps.'

We rumbled into the dirty depression of Goole and turned south-east for Scunthorpe. The sun was behind us, the road across the flat fenland was devoid of interest. Another brief moment of contentment was over.

Felton was older than me. In spite of our acquaintance over two or three years, I knew little about him. Our common interest was aircraft and ships: his deep, mine superficial. I had never had close friends; and now he was extending both hands in friendship, I was not interested. Yet he had certainly proved to be a friend in need at Barton. Was my inner reasoning wrong? Should I grasp at this straw which floated so temptingly close?

As we droned along the flat, featureless fen road to Keadby Bridge I recognised that although I may not always be right, certainly my choice of life was no more wrong than anybody else's. This was not the time to abandon our voyage. We would, we *must*, go on. Ahead were limitless horizons; here there would be a great emptiness, like the very fens themselves.

'It's a long road from Goole,' I commented.

'And dreary,' agreed Felton. 'Nothing to see.'

11. THIRD START LUCKY

Felton was not generous to a fault: I earned my living. We moved bricks and tiles, and sundry pieces of hardware, and plenty of soft goods; we dumped rubble on farm roads and levelled them; we carried slag, and collected dried beet pulp. Sometimes I delivered alone in Felton's other lorry, an ancient ex-Army truck. It was interesting work and it made a little money—enough to live on.

In between trips and jobs I worked on my new topmast. I borrowed a draw-knife from one of the shipwrights at the boat yard and stripped the bark from my tree. Apart from smoothing the surface clear of the knots which stood proud, and adzing the required 'D' shape at the foot to fit the hounds, I dared not remove any more strength from the willowy spar. Instead of cutting the intricate cavern into the heel which would accommodate the self-tripping fid, I bored straight through with a screw-auger and fitted a 1-inch bolt. The spider-band at the hounds (to which was shackled the topsail and staysail halliards) could not be settled on a joggle, because the mast just wasn't thick enough at that point; I drove it into position with a maul and ensured that it would not slip down further when the wet wood dried by screwing oak 'stops' on either side of the mast. The 6-foot pole I painted red; the golden truck, fortunately, fitted over the end without difficulty. I painted the bottom section, 'twixt mainmast cap and hounds, white, as before, but decided that black paint was unlikely to last long on the hoist of this very wet spar. I would grease it thoroughly once it was on board and in position, which should lock the moisture in and retain maximum strength through flexibility.

Kester and I went through the whole miserable business again of part-lowering the mainmast. Somehow, the two of us struggled our new topmast aboard and heaved it upwards, with numerous tackles, levers and wedges, into position. Then, clinging periously to the steeply-angled mast (the topmast would not pass under the forestay if the mast was fully lowered, and once fitted I did not want to lower right down because it all had to be heaved up again), I greased the unpainted centre section of our new spar, using water-resisting pump grease.

Clank by slow clank we—Kester, Mollie and I—hove up the gear. Then I went aloft and screwed the pole which bore our table-cloth/parachute-silk bob, rove off the halliards and seated the shrouds. Kester and I hoisted the topmast and set up the shrouds. Finally, as before, we rigged the topsail and the stay-sail. Once again *J & M* was ready for sea. And it was from exactly then that I added a new worry to my ever-growing list: could that much-too-slender-and-ever-so-whippy spar survive a blow?

All the work was accomplished, bit by bit, over four weeks. We hove up on the evening of 7 June, as a sort of birthday present for me, and after that it was Whit weekend.

It was a suitable moment for Kester to leave school once again.

I would have liked to sail right away. Much as I had enjoyed our visit to the little Haven, the long wait had been a strain on the nerves. It is a very phoney pleasure to live in limbo, but with a minimum of money and a maximum of difficulties to solve, limbo can be hell on earth. Live, simultaneously, in a miniature sort of paradise, however, and one soon begins to lose one's identity and purpose. Why go on when one can lotus-eat here? Why worry when every day will produce a new unsolvable problem, which will be resolved automatically by the simple process of just hanging around and waiting for something to happen. At Barton Haven I learned a little about the mental deterioration which evolves a beachcomber. It is not a difficult trade.

'Darling,' I said to Mollie, when the topmast was up, the topsail tested by hoisting, and my ship was once again a-tauto, 'we must get away from this place just as soon as we can. I've got a couple of day's work painting Felton's house. I'd better not go up there on Whit Monday, so I'll be finished on Wednesday. Thursday is the 13th, and I'm not particularly bothered about that, but the market-boat doesn't come in until Friday. So let's get ready to go out on Friday the 14th.'

Mollie said, a little anxiously: 'Alone?'

'Well you don't want Len and Felton again do you?'

'No.' And then womanlike: 'But can we handle her by ourselves?'

'We've done it before; we intended to do it any rate before Len and Felton turned up. We'll just bloody well *have* to do it.'

Kester said stoutly: 'Of *course* we can do it.'

It was a conference of a sort—without alternatives.

To our surprise, Felton turned up on Sunday evening with yet another bottle of wine.

'I thought you might be feeling fed up,' was his excuse. 'I expect you could do with a drink.'

I had to admit that lack of money had prevented me from indulging one of my only two vices: beer before lunch, and pipe-smoking. Of these, reluctantly, I had had to forgo the beer—apart from an occasional couple of pints after a particularly hard morning. I didn't like wine, but it was better than nothing.

'Thanks,' I said, but I didn't really mean it. Once a decision to set forth in a boat has been made, discussions with outsiders tend to disturb the slow build-up of resolution. I wanted us to be left alone; I sensed that Mollie and Kester, too, felt as I did.

I told him that we hoped to leave on Friday.

'A bad day, Friday,' he said. 'It's supposed to be unlucky to sail on a Friday. Why not leave it until next week and then I'll be able to come with you, and I expect I shall be able to persuade Len to come too. I know his wife is a bit anti, but in the circumstances . . .'

'No!' I almost shouted. 'It's very nice of you, Felton, but we must get cracking as soon as possible. I had a visit from a River

Board official last week, and although he was very nice about
our being here he pointed out that as they'd had a complaint
they must react to it. I told him that we'd be leaving this week
and he was quite happy. I don't want to put their backs up by
staying longer.'

'What a pity.' Felton shook his head. 'Well, I'll see if I can
arrange things so that I can join you on Friday. Let me see—'
He broke off to investigate his mental files of work in hand.

'Felton,' I began, about to stagger into the first excuse of why
we didn't want either him or Len. . . . But he went on without
noticing my interruption.

'No,' he said positively, 'I just can't make it. What a pity!
I've got that new contract, and I daren't miss out one of the runs
now. What a shame! But I'll try and find somebody else to
come if you like.'

'No, Felton. Really, We can cope. We've sailed her before
by ourselves you know.'

'Yes, but not down two hundred miles of harbourless coastline.' he replied promptly, and of course he was right. 'You
really ought to have a bigger crew.' And he was right again.

'Oh, we'll cope,' I said airily in an effort to stop his frantic
do-gooding, although I knew that I was talking tripe. Cope we
would have to—but it wasn't going to be easy; cope with
another crew—no!

Painting Felton's house had been his idea, since work with
the lorry tailed off and the odd trip had not warranted the
expense of a driver's mate. It was a straightforward job: a quick
rub down and a two-in-one topcoat. Not my idea of a good
finish, but that was what Felton wanted and he was paying. His
house overlooked the river from the low rise to the west of the
town which was the northern extremity of the optimistically-
named Lincolnshire Heights. Neither the position nor the
newness of the house surprised me—both were so obviously
what one would expect of Felton.

His wife was pleasant enough, but I had not been there long
before she brought me a cup of coffee and began to talk. She
did not have to chatter long before I was fully informed about

her hopes and fears. Perhaps I am a sympathetic listener; perhaps she seldom had a chance to unload her worries (for the new house was quite isolated, one of the first of a new estate).

Felton, it seemed, was discontented with his lot: he wanted to get out—but he did not know how to do it. He thought that Mollie, Kester and I were leading the perfect life. He had wanted to sell out and buy a boat and live afloat ever since he had first visited us on *J & M*. And she was worried. Our present close proximity had re-energised his determination to get away from it all. Even now—at that moment—she suspected that Felton was trying to sell his new lorry.

'But he must be daft,' I exclaimed. 'He's got a good little business and plenty of time to ship-spot or do whatever he likes.'

'I'm afraid,' she said, 'that you are the evil influence.'

And it's not the first time, I thought.

I told her then that we were going on Friday and that we were going alone. 'Once we leave,' I suggested, 'he'll probably settle down again.'

'If he hasn't sold his lorry this morning,' she sighed, 'there may be a chance.'

Felton turned up just before I left for *J & M*. He had not sold his lorry, and I judged it imprudent to say anything about my conversation with his wife.

'See you tomorrow,' was my parting remark.

And so on the following day, I finished the painting and I said goodbye. I never saw them again. A brief ray of light had, in different ways, inter-illuminated the Mixford and the Clarke families; now it was snuffed, and no doubt the grey gloom of the everlasting rut was as depressing to Felton as was our loss of the temporary security of kindness and help which he unstintingly gave to us.

On the Thursday there was a lot to do. Mollie shopped, Kester carried, I loaded anthracite and water and checked over all the gear for the last time. Once again, the sickness of premeditated action loosened my bowels and the fear of what we were about to attempt distorted my thinking. Over and over again I went through the process of *J & M* being towed stern-first out of the Haven like a bad tooth being pulled. At each think, something terrible happened. I did not spare myself the horrible details.

I had passed the word to *Khama's* skipper, and I had learned that he would be off *J & M's* stern at eight. We rose at six-thirty, ate a hearty breakfast (like criminals about to die!), and were ready by seven-thirty. We singled-up the mooring warps, trundled the gangplank on board and stowed it between the skylights on the main hatch, coiled our best towing rope aft with a heaving line ready for action, topped-up the port spreader (an overhead gantry on the Maltings could have fouled our rigging if we accidentally sheered the wrong way), released the kicking strap which prevents the rudder from banging about when the barge is at anchor or moored, sheeted out the topsail, prepared the foresail for quick release, uncleated the inner and outer, and upper and lower brails. . . . And now we were ready.

It was not a bad morning for a start. The weather forecast had given moderate north-easterly winds, cloudy at first with the sun breaking through later in the morning. Even as *Khama* pulled away from the landing place on the opposite side of the Haven, the sun suddenly shafted a pool of localised warmth and comfort over our deck. *Khama* turned, bows pointed sea-wards through the narrow gap between the golden sandbank and the Maltings, and then she came astern towards us.

Khama's mate flung a heaving line. Swiftly I fastened it to our warp and watched the 6-inch rope snake over the taffrail as the mate hauled it across and dropped the loop over their stern bollard. I pulled a bight under the main-horse, slipped it over the horse chock, and waved all ready. The water erupted under *Khama's* stern. Kester had already released our stern mooring; now he slipped our bow warp. I lifted the fid from the wheel, and facing aft I concentrated on negotiating the narrow exit from Barton Haven.

As when we came, the disturbance to the muddy waters erupted the filthy putrescence into an overpowering stench

which contrasted sadly with the temporary shaft of sunlight which lit our departure. A few onlookers at the boatyard and the Maltings waved goodbye as I steered a straight course through the narrow exit (much to my surprise she handled beautifully). We waved back.

And then we were outside our miniature paradise, and *Khama* was tooting to let go the stern tow, and the sun was cut out abruptly by more dark clouds, and *Khama* was alongside our port bow handing over the warp for refastening, and then going ahead towards Hull with *J & M* in tow; and I was hoisting the topsail whilst Mollie steered, and lowering the port leeboard, and setting the mainsail, and heaving in the released tow, and waving my grateful thanks to *Khama*, and setting the foresail, and the mizzen, and checking that the skiff was towing and hadn't fouled anything. . . .

And worrying all the time about whether we would be able to complete the voyage which lay ahead; and wondering where our next landfall would be and how we could survive on the paltry sum which was all that was left after our stay in Barton Haven. . . .

We had food for a week, emergency rations for a month, and sixteen shillings in the kitty. But we were clear, at last, from Lincolnshire, from interference and from civilisation!

I went to the wheel and put *J & M* on the starboard tack, adjusted the wangs, and then filled my pipe and lit up. *Khama* was already a mile away, heading directly for Hull. Once again the sun broke through the overcast. It was going to be a fine day with a fair breeze by the looks of things. I was still worried —but not unhappy.

12. FIRST DAY

When *Khama* dropped the tow at 0810 hours, the tide had just
begun to ebb and the wind was light north-easterly. The sun
continued to break up the clouds until, after an hour, it shone
from cloudless blue skies. It was a comfortable enough beginning.

The wind was so light that it took some time to sail across
the Humber to the north bank, heading upstream as we had
done on the disastrous setting forth six weeks before. But this
time the fast ebb tide was sweeping us seawards, so that we
were below Barton Haven when we finally reached the
opposite side.

'You take the bowlin',' I told Mollie, 'and you stay aft and
hang on to Sym;' I said to Kester. He remonstrated, but I was
firm: 'Don't argue. I'm not going to risk you or Sym getting
hurt. Your job is to look after him, and the best place is aft—so
every time we go about you must stay here with him. O.K.?'

Grumpily, Kester agreed.

'Ready about,' I shouted to Mollie. 'Lee-O.'

In the light breeze, *J & M* winded slowly. I had ample time
to drop the starboard leeboard and hoist the weather 'board. I
trimmed the port wang and went back to the wheel.

'We really need the stays'l,' I said, half to myself.

'Good idea. I'll take the wheel,' Kester butted in.

'Now wait a minute. Don't be so ruddy keen.'

I knew that the staysail was essential, but after our last effort,
and now with this new whippy topmast, I was not all that
anxious to commit myself.

'Darling,' I called to Mollie, 'will you take the wheel for a
bit?'

There was the next problem. Mollie could handle a sailing dinghy as well as anybody, but *J & M* frightened her and somehow she seemed unable to hold a reasonable course—either on or off the wind. Kester had had no previous experience at steering the barge, because he was only five when he sailed in her last. Mollie came reluctantly to the wheel.

'Don't be scared of it,' I encouraged, but she gripped the spokes too determinedly and I sensed her fear. 'I'll have to give her the stays'l—otherwise we'll be all day getting down the river. Just keep her on this course, that's all. You stay here, Kes.'

I went to the staysail and unfastened the three stops which lashed it to the starboard rail. I checked that the tails of the two sheets were made fast and then, none too happily, I hauled away at the halliard. Flogging gently, the white sail crept up the topmast forestay. I cleated the halliard, and struggled to sheet in the sail as much as possible; as the wind was light, I managed to get most of it. Then I went to the stem-head and bowsed down the tack. As I worked, I looked aloft at the topmast: it showed no sign of distortion, although, of course, there was hardly enough wind to cause trouble as yet.

I suddenly realised that we were luffing. 'Bear away! Bear away!' I shouted to Mollie, and ran back to the wheel which she handed over to me with obvious relief.

"It's no good. I just can't get used to this damn' thing,' she said.

'Not to worry.' I tried to keep cheerful as I hastily revised my orders. 'Kes can look after the bowlin' next time we tack, if you'll take the stays'l sheet. There's not much wind, and once we're round the bend off Hull we should be able to lay a course straight down the river.'

But how, I wondered to myself, are we going to get on if the wind increases?

We made the next tack successfully. Kester left the bowline on the shroud and released the staysail sheet, whilst Mollie overhauled the lee staysail sheet and tightened it as much as she could. As usual, I downed and upped the leeboards. The timing

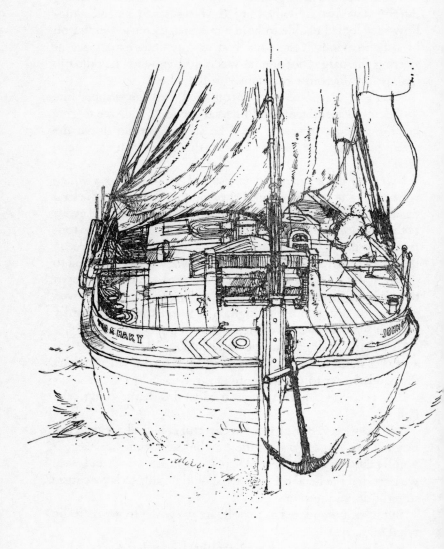

was not too bad in the light wind. 'Let draw!' I shouted to
Kester, and he released the bowline after he finished helping his
mother with the staysail.

Sym, surprisingly, had been very obedient and stayed aft
when I told him.

I felt just a little more confident.

It seemed that in less than no time we were winding off Hull
docks, and the almost straight reach for the sea lay before us.
Now the tide would really help us on our way. If we could
arrive off Donna Nook by low water—a distance of twenty
five miles—the late afternoon flood would sweep us towards
the Wash—but I was doubtful if we would make it in the
light breeze.

Mollie went below to begin her preparations for lunch, and
Kester (after asking my permission) took Sym to his favourite
position forward between the bitts, from where he could look
down the stem at the bubbling bow wave. Sym spent five
minutes forward, sitting bolt upright and examining the gentle
off-shore breeze with his fastidious nostrils, and then decided
that the temptations of the shore were more than he could bear;
he came aft and whined to be allowed below, and I left the
wheel to give him the necessary help.

I judged the wind had been just about Force 4, but I felt sure
that it was dropping. We were close-hauled on the port tack
but although all our sails were drawing, *J & M* was noticeably
sagging towards the south bank although I was doing everything possible to hold her up to windward. I suspected that the
current was responsible, but I also feared that the wind might
be slowly veering. Not an easterly, I prayed—not a bloody
dead muzzler all the way to Great Yarmouth. Yet there was no
doubt that the wind was slowly heading us.

I watched our gently fluttering bob and almost continually
checked the flow of the sails; at frequent intervals, I dropped
the fid on the wheel and walked to leeward to lean out over the
iron handrail and peer round the mainsail: there was a lot of
movement on the river and I didn't want to get foul of any
craft—or athwart any buoys.

KB

Humber buoys are rather unique. Because of the wicked current, the usual navigation marks would never stay on the surface when the river was in full spate—they would strain to the limit of their mooring, and then they would be dragged under. So Humber buoys are 20-foot double-ended steel boats, flush-decked, like miniature lightships. I had been so intrigued with them when we had arrived at Barton that I decided to scull out in the barge skiff to investigate. I had set out one afternoon an hour before high water. Sculling lazily upstream with the current I covered the two miles to the nearest buoy in about twenty minutes. With a smooth rush of water like this one does not notice the swift approach of danger. One minute, I was turning the skiff to head into the current, the next I was alongside the boat-buoy's bow-wave and flashing past almost too quickly to grab hold. Even when I caught a turn of the painter over a bollard, the sudden strain was so great that I was nearly jerked off my feet; the bows of the skiff rose as it too battled against the mill-race current.

With this experience in mind, I was almighty careful never to wind within three or four hundred yards up-current of any buoy or boat-buoy on the Humber. The thought of what would happen if we fouled one was too appalling to contemplate. The secret of *J & M*'s near-capsize off Barton was also still too frighteningly fresh in my mind! From Barton to Grimsby I stuck to the marked channel as rigidly as if I had been conning the *Queen Mary*.

Our first board down the long reach took us very nearly to Immingham Docks. I made my decision in ample time as to where I would wind, and called out to Mollie to come and stand by. Kester stretched himself up from his comfortable nook and went to the bowline. Nearly an hour had passed, and already our ship was divided into three areas of silent pre-occupation—plus an additional two smaller areas for Sym and Tigger. As skipper, I had to break up these routines, but each time I was forced into the realisation that we were now living two lives at the same time. There was the sailing ship *J & M*, and the houseboat *J & M*: I had the one, and Mollie had the other. Kester helped in both, and Sym and Tigger were with Mollie. It was an odd situation.

We winded nicely, but as Mollie turned to go below I warned her that this would be a short tack.

'Hell!' she said. 'I've got something cooking on the Rayburn.'

'Well we'll have to go about again in five minutes.'

'All right. I'll come up then.'

Two different worlds. . . .

This was the losing tack—badly so. We were very nearly stemming the current as we slanted across the river towards the north bank which was now the north-east bank.

'Ready about!' I bawled to Mollie, and had to wait in desperation until she had climbed on deck via the fo'c's'le hatch and stood by the staysail sheet.

'Lee-O.'

The next making leg was not nearly as long as the first. As we passed Immingham, the channel curved slightly more into wind. Within minutes we had to tack again . . . and then again. . . . Holme Ridge boat-buoy was just to windward, marking the kink in the river, and I watched it anxiously as the tide swept J & M down towards it. If I could weather this mark, the channel would allow me to sail almost across to the north-east shore. But as is so often the case when tacking in strong tides and confined waters, ship and buoy were attracting each other. I would not risk it: I winded again.

This making leg just enabled me to lay clear of Grimsby, and at last I could tell Mollie that I would not be needing her on deck for a while. She went below, and Kester resumed his bow position—then the wind seemed to freshen a little.

Now that we were past Immingham, the vast area of Sunk Sand inside Spurn Head opened up to windward. This probably accounted for the wind freshening. To J & M it was still only a breeze, but to our faithful skiff, towing astern, the wind-against-tide was raising a lop which began a plunge-jerk-smash action. I knew that this could easily turn into a disaster if the 2½-inch painter snapped. I would have to hoist the skiff in the davits. Once again I called for Mollie. Once again the interruption was an irritation.

It took me half an hour to drag the skiff alongside the port quarter, make fast, climb down and hook on the tackles, heave the bows clear of the water, then the stern ... and then, inch by inch, with Kester adding his slight weight to the best of his ability, sweating on those falls until the skiff was fully raised block-and-block. I passed two lines around her hull and bound her securely to the davits, so that she could not crash about when the barge rolled. Then I relieved Mollie at the helm, stepping over that cursed sludge pump on the port quarter-deck for the hundredth time!

'Can I get on with lunch now,' she asked sarcastically.

I looked aloft at the bob, the sails, and then fidded the wheel to peer round the mainsail to leeward. We were just about holding our own.

'Yes, O.K.' I said. 'I don't think we'll have to tack again.'

We didn't. But it was a thankless task preventing *J & M* from sagging to leeward towards Grimsby pier-heads. The wind, having had its bit of fun, naturally began to falter. It died very very gradually until it was difficult to know whether the current or the wind was helping most. Slowly but successfully we weathered the pier-heads—not too close fortunately, as otherwise I would have been forced to get Mollie on deck again and make another board—but when we were past, the wind barely gave us steerage way and I knew from the start that very soon we were going to be swept over the Clee Ness Sand.

'What's the time?' I called to Mollie, her answer came, muffled, from below: 'Just gone two.' I was absolutely staggered; I thought it was probably just approching midday.

This meant that it was very nearly low water here, so it would not really matter if we did run aground. I searched the blue skies for any sign of wind, but the hot sun had dried them clear. We could go aground in safety. If we just cleared the sands, so much the better—the nearer we could get to Donna Nook before the tide turned, the greater the advantage to us. But to tack now, in almost slack water, would be a waste of time. We were as well-off here as anywhere.

Mollie put her head through the after companionway and asked: 'What are you going to do about lunch? I'd better give Kester his first.'

'I'll have mine at the wheel,' I told her. 'There's hardly any wind, but I'd prefer to stay on deck.'

'All right. Come on, Kes, lunch up,' she called.

Kester uncurled from the foredeck and went below through the fo'c's'le hatch. I was left alone on deck.

It was then I discovered that we were no longer sailing. The wind had died so very gradually, and the tide had slackened so imperceptibly, it was quite possible that we hadn't so much run aground as dropped the last inch or so vertically when the last of the ebb left us. Even the leeboard pendant had given no warning. I poked the short hitcher (boat-hook) over the side: yes, we were hard and fast. I watched the water alongside: there was just a slight drift of current seawards. I looked at the bob: it was very nearly limp, with just an occasional weak stirring. I looked all around: Spurn Head lighthouse showed up clearly to the north-east, and the yellow sands of Cleethorpes extended endlessly under our starboard beam. Not a ship or a boat was anywhere near; my barge was safe enough for half an hour or so. I went forward and lowered the staysail, lashing it as usual to the starboard wire hand-rail. I dropped the anchor, and let out a couple of fathoms of chain. Then I went below to enjoy my lunch in comfort.

We floated again just before three. A sudden rattle, a faint stirring, and I hurried on deck via the after cabin. We had floated and swung, bows pointing offshore. J & M had indicated that she was ready to go. The bob, even as I watched, stirred its swallow-tail, flicked, dusted around, flapped gently, and then lifted as a cool breeze whispered around my ears. I twisted my head from side to side, sensing the exact direction and checking it with the bob. The breeze was from the east-north-east—

barely fair. I looked to windward at the blue placid estuary waters, but there were as yet no signs of the breeze increasing.

Without disturbing Kester, who was wiping up for Mollie, I went to the windlass and checked the lay of the anchor cable. Then I gave *J & M* a sheer on the helm, put the foresail hard aback on the bowline, and cranked up the anchor. It broke out without effort. We were under way again.

By the time Kester came on deck with Sym (bundled up the after companion-way by Mollie), we were on course for Donna Nook—just able to lay the point.

'Shall we set the staysail again?' Kester wanted to know.

I looked to windward again. A smoky haze had crept across the horizon, and already the advancing breeze had ruffled the surface of the estuary to a darker hue. There were only wavelets at present, but I knew that very soon the breeze would become a wind, and the sea would get up.

'No, Kes,' I told him. 'We'll soon be getting as much wind as we need.'

Within an hour it was blowing Force 5. The gentle waters of the lunch period had gone, and now the seas were short and steep and carried white horses on many of their backs. It was an ideal barge wind. If I had had a crew, I would have revelled in the beat to windward, but crippled as I was, in my usual manner I began to worry. Force 5 was not too bad, especially if we did not have to tack, but I hoped that it would not increase further.

In a surprisingly short time we passed No. 2 D.Z. buoy which marked Donna Nook point. We were so pinched that I could not weather it, so we rounded close to leeward. The sea-gull-whitened conical mark rolled and dipped to us as we sped by, making, I guessed, seven knots. Directly we were round I eased the helm half a point so that we were no longer pinching to windward—and I relaxed slightly as we freed our wind. I showed Kester on the chart where the next buoy should appear and he went forward with the binoculars to spot for me. Sym was not interested, and whined to go below to Mollie. I fidded the wheel, lowered him down, filled my pipe and lit up; then I did my best to settle down to the rhythm of the sea.

J & M did not have a binnacle. I had a boxed ex-RAF compass, but I had no idea of what deviation it would suffer from the various hunks of iron around the steering position (including the mangle-type wheel), and so I relied more on my instincts than technical navigation. Now that we were clear of the constricting Humber, I tried to take a few transit bearings, using the chart. Judging the exact bearing with the compass on the deck was well-nigh impossible, but as far as I could see all the hunks of iron neutralised each other: the compass was vaguely accurate enough for my purposes.

I had on many previous occasions been slated for my seemingly nonchalant approach to navigation—both air- and seaborne. As a pupil-pilot I had always been amazed at the detailed preparation which most of my fellow cadets made before a cross-country flight—and yet in spite of this many of them often managed to get themselves lost. Mumbling such 'reminders' as: 'Deviation west: compass best', and juggling with drift, course-correction, ETA, variation, and 'keeping red on red', I was never surprised when they succeeded in confusing themselves so much that some managed to steer a reciprocal course into the wild blue yonder, which inevitably meant a forced landing in the remotest and most inaccessible spot they could discover.

I preferred to stick to the simple method which I suspected animals and birds used—that of orientation from known sea- or landmarks or from the position of the sun. I had read stories about bargemen and fishermen who seemingly could find their way in thick fog by the sounds and smells around them, and from the sight and *taste* of what an armed lead brought up from the bottom. I discovered, after some practice, that the system worked.

I was not cranky about it; I am not a flat-earther; I have many navigational successes to prove my point. On one occasion, when sandwiched between two layers of ten-tenths cloud, my aircraft was riddled by a burst of unexpected fire from a Ju 88; without radio or compass I found my aerodrome, although the cloud was down to three hundred feet and lying on the nearby hills. Another time I led five aircraft on an attack against an enemy airstrip across two hundred and fifty miles of naked and unmapped desert. I had to repeat this little effort twice because only one other pilot out of many attempts could find the place.

And so I had reasoned that automatic navigational ability worked along the same lines as telling the time when you have never owned a watch. I hadn't—but, day or night, I was seldom more than ten minutes out in my guess.

In any case, with the best will in the world, I had not had enough money to set up a proper binnacle and have *J & M* swung by a compass adjuster. I had purchased six up-to-date charts which covered every eventuality on our proposed route, I had a lead and line, and there was a compass on board which could be useful in the doubtful event of a thick sea mist. I had all the essentials. Just before we sailed there was a report from Hull that one of their trawlers, crammed with navigational aids, had piled up on a Scottish headland. It ain't the ships, it's the men in 'em.

Then there had been the nagging problem of which route to follow. On one of my many trips with Felton, we had spotted Bob Robert's coasting barge *Cambria* lying by Keadby Bridge and we had stopped for a chat. Bob, as professional as ever, had advised me to go off-shore, round the Dowsings. 'You want to keep away from the Burnham Flats,' he had said. 'A nasty place to be if the wind gets up.' Of course, in his case he was right—but this advice did not take our peculiar circumstanes into consideration.

I knew that *J & M* would start to leak again. I also knew that I had a weak crew (physically—not in determination). I argued to myself that if we followed the coast—the dangerous overland route across the Burnham Flats—I could always, as a last resort, beach *J & M* anywhere on the gently shelving shores and Mollie and Kester could step ashore almost without getting wet. It was a desperate last-measure thought, which would almost inevitably mean the total loss of our home and all our belongings, but it had given me some comfort in my lonely thinking.

Now, with the wind as it was, I had no alternative. We were pinned to a lee-shore by wind and tide, and even if I had come to a decision it was now quite impractical for us to head towards deep water. Grouse you may, whined the wind in our rigging, but go you must! We pounded onwards towards the overland route.

And we were certainly pounding!

No sailing vessel likes working to windward, and no helmsman can really enjoy the rigid concentration which is so necessary if the ship is going to get anywhere at all. Oh, some profess delight in yacht racing—'A good thrash to wind'ard,' they'll say, 'is a wonderful experience'—and no doubt an hour or two is quite good fun; but at best a barge is an indifferent windward performer because of her flat bottom, and certainly no helmsman should be expected to steer along a lee-shore in such conditions hour after hour after hour.

When each white-capped wave met the tarred breakwater of *J & M*'s port bow, it jerked her slightly off-course as the bows lifted, and a few droplets of spray were flung over Kester's head. Slowly the stem would continue to rise and swing to leeward until—slam!—the bows dropped suddenly when the wave passed aft. There would follow a sideways wriggle and a caterpillar-like ripple as *J & M* corkscrewed over the angle of the passing sea, and by then the bows would be meeting the next wave. The motion necessitated constant helm action. It was difficult to find spare seconds to light my pipe.

By five o'clock I knew that it would be prudent to rig the lee rolling wang, for the windward roll at the passing of each wave was sufficient to jerk the spreet part-way amidships against the pressure of wind, and the next roll to starboard smashed it to leeward until it was brought up all-standing with an audible THUD! against the port wang. Kester knew how to rig the tackle, and I watched him closely as he unfastened the end of the starboard rolling wang from the foot of the spreet,

passed it outside the starboard topmast backstay, runners and
shrouds, hooked on the tackle (which was always kept stowed
on the fore-hatch when at sea), slackened off the fall until the
figure-of-eight knot was jammed against the upper block,
hooked the lower block to the chain-plate outside the rail and
just abaft the curve of the bow, and overhauled the fall as much
as he was able. Then I fidded the wheel, ran forward, waited
until *J & M* lurched to starboard, hove as tight as I could at the
exact moment of slack, caught a turn around the cleat inside
the rail—once round, two crosses, a loose half-hitch—and sped
back to the wheel in time to check the next swing of the
plunging bows. Over the next hour I had to tighten the tackle
four times as the new rope stretched to the strain, but the
ominous thudding of spreet against weather wang was under
control and *J & M* no longer shivered from the shocks.

Whether the effort involved was responsible, or perhaps it
was the corkscrew motion, I don't know, but from the wheel I
could sense that Kester—who had returned to his look-out
position in the bows—was not feeling well. I fidded the wheel
again, and ran forward. 'Do you feel sick?' I asked him.

He lifted a wan face and told me 'No!', quite firmly, but he
was obviously just on the verge.

'Come on aft,' I said, and called to Mollie.

When she poked her head up through the after-cabin hatch,
I could see that she, too, was not right.

'Sym's been sick,' she told me.

'How about you?'

'I'm all right.'

'Tigger?'

'Oh, he couldn't care less. He's asleep.'

'Kester's a bit crook,' I said, 'and you don't look too good.
Could you brew up some tea?'

'I've just made some.'

'Good.'

I made Kester sit to leeward on the quarter-deck, and when
Mollie handed up steaming mugs of tea I suggested that she did
the same. Sym was much too miserable to want to join them,

and I saw him clamber laboriously on to the starboard bunk in the after cabin where he squirmed himself into a tight ball, nose on tail, to eye me with reproachful misgivings.

An hour later, with some dry arrowroot biscuit and more tea to help, both Mollie and Kester felt a lot better. It was as well: I had been wondering what I would do with a seasick crew on my hands.

At around six, when they were still huddled on the quarter-deck, I sensed that the wind was increasing. I said nothing: they had enough to do trying to gain their sea-legs. But I could not fool Mollie.

'Isn't the wind stronger?' she asked, and scrambled to her feet to gaze anxiously to windward and then upwards to our bob.

'Just a bit.'

'We're not in for a gale . . .?'

'How's the bilge?' I asked her, changing the subject. I had not wanted to disturb them whilst they were so comfortable, and now I had missed the weather forecast. Maybe there had been a gale warning for the east coast.

'I'll go and have a look.'

Kester went below with her.

Anxiety was brewing again, and I wanted to keep it at bay for as long as possible.

'Kes. Tell Mollie to make another pot of tea,' I said as he went down the ladder.

Alone once more on the deck, with the warmth of the sun beginning to fade as it dropped towards the shore horizon, I shivered in anticipation of what the night would bring. I was in no doubt now that the wind had increased to Force 6: the bob stood straight out, our spindly new topmast bowed to the strain of the bulging topsail, wangs and sheets were bar-taut, we had an average 15-degree list to starboard and seldom came completely upright at the end of every roll.

Force 6 at six, Force 7 at seven, Force 8 at eight, I began thinking. . . .

J & M pitched and rolled and corkscrewed onwards towards

her unplanned destination, taking us with her to our unknown destiny.

By the time Mollie had brewed a second pot of tea, we had been on the go for twelve hours and I had been at the helm for more than ten of them. We were about to cross the Wash; when darkness came we would be somewhere in the heaving confusion of seas over Burnham Flats which, if the wind stayed at Force 6, were the next inevitable hazard. Mollie reported that the bilge had not yet risen very much over the sealing; Kester reported that he didn't feel sick any more—'Well, not very much.' Everything was just hanging by a thread; everybody was trying to be too normal.

J & M reared and plunged to the rhythm of the seas and ignored our futile gestures of bravery.

She couldn't care bloody less.

13. FIRST NIGHT

To sit for hours at the helm of a monster over which one has little control, and yet be aware of every tiny weakness and fault because one has laboured so conscientiously in order to make that monster work as efficiently and as safely as possible, is a miserable torture. On the one hand, *J & M* was going south and taking us with her: we were entirely supernumary; on the other, I could not dismiss from my mind the knowledge of her complete inability to survive a major battle against nature in her sixtieth year without help.

I wondered whether I should ease her load: part-brail the mainsail, or ruck the topsail (i.e. drop the peak, and use only the lower sheeted portion of sail). But although she was pounding across the Wash, shouldering occasional spray across her foredeck, I could not really bring myself to believe that she was labouring. The wind, too, was a strong but steady Force 6— no squalls, and no signs of increasing strength. So I worried alone—and let her get on with her voyage. But I had to work hard at the helm to keep her on course: she couldn't go on her way entirely unaided!

I thought of possible ducking grounds—anchorages behind banks, or easily entered creeks—but even as I thought, *J & M* ploughed onwards across the Wash towards the next lee-shore, and I was leaving the only possible shelter, Boston Deep, far away under our starboard quarter. Before darkness fell we reached the Burnham Flat buoy, and entered the overland route.

Mollie had been busy below for some time—getting Kester to bed in the after cabin, I assumed. The sun had not so much

gone down as just faded away: the purple twilight deepening
imperceptibly, and the seas darkening from foam-flecked blue,
to grey, to black. The gradual process gave the impression of an
approaching storm, and the realism was aided by a vast bank of
black cloud which built up over the land which now lay

directly ahead, and the ugly, white-crested waves which surged
and tumbled to windward of us. Overhead, the stars began to
prick through the last of the blue sky over the sea; ahead the
twinkle of an occasional shore light showed against the black
background.

And *J & M* reared and shuddered, and rolled and corkscrewed over the shallow waters of the overland route, pointing in the general direction of Blakeney. She might, I thought

—and how I hoped that she would—just clear the headland towards Sheringham; but I knew that the tide had turned, and that it would be forcing our bows inshore towards—I looked at at the chart—Wells. It was eleven miles from the Burnham Flat buoy to Holkham Bay, and it was going to be an unhappy slog against wind and tide all the way.

I remembered then, too late for Kester to help, that I had not lit the navigation lights. I thought of calling to Mollie, but I knew that as she had not come on deck then she must be busy: a light glowed through the galley skylight to show where she was. Kester had set up the port and starboard light boards on their tall iron posts during the afternoon, and I remembered that he had filled the lamps before we left Ferriby. I judged the best spoke to leave the wheel, fidded it, and watched the bows for a few seconds to see if she was reasonably settled enough to hold her course for a minute or so. Twice I had to adjust the wheel by one notch. When she seemed reasonably happy, I ran forward, lifted the fo'c's'le hatch, and scrambled below.

As I grabbed the first lamp which came to hand in the gloom —it was the starboard one—and swung open the back door (those lighthouses of galvanised iron could not possibly be said to have anything else but an inspection *door*—hinged as it was with brass, with a brass door handle), slid out the container and chimney, and fumbled for a match, I became gradually conscious of the entirely different world inside the hull.

At first, with the sudden cessation of the noises of wind and sea, it was as hushed as a tomb. Then the bubbling gurgle of foam passing down each side of the bows, followed by an irregular *thud* as each wave was smashed aside, became apparent. Next, a continual sloshing of bilge water was evident, with an awe-inspiring *woo-o-sh*! every so often as a sudden flip roll jerked the lot to leeward. Sundry raps and rattlings told of bar-taut halliards and straining blocks beating against spars, and the many creaks and grinds were an ominous indication of how hard my barge was working. But of all the noises, the bilge woosh scared me most: it could not be seen forward because we were six inches by the stern, but the sound was enough. . . .

As I listened, I worked. Off chimney, up wick, light. On chimney, carefully adjust wick, slide in container, shut back door. I climbed the ladder, humping the heavy lamp carefully through the narrow hatch, and stumbled as quickly as possible to leeward. I hefted the lamp over the lightboard, positioned it carefully on the retaining hook, and slid it into position. A quick look from forward to check that the light was burning brightly, and then I ran quickly back to the wheel. I had been, perhaps, ninety seconds; I was just in time to prevent *J & M* from luffing hard into wind.

Sailing barges vary enormously in how long they can hold a course without anybody at the helm. Long straight chines are generally better at this than the bow-to-stern curved chine which *J & M* had. Given light winds and calm seas she could just about maintain five minutes of uninterrupted self-steering —once she had managed eight—but in weather like this, one to two minutes was the best I could expect.

After the gloom of the fo'c's'le, the twilight seemed almost day, but as I settled down at the helm for a few minutes before lighting the port lamp, darkness crept over the ship so that I could no longer see clearly the chart which was spread out on the coachroof abaft the wheel. Now the brightness from the galley skylight was affecting my night sight.

'Darling,' I called, and then louder. 'Darling.' I stepped over the main-horse and bashed the top of the coachroof.

The glow of the lamp in the galley faded, swelled through the saloon skylights, and then disappeared as Mollie ducked into the after cabin. A pause, and then her head appeared through the hatch, lit from below and half-behind by the now-turned-down Aladdin which she had stood on the cabin table.

'Is Kester in bed?' I asked.

'He's been in about half-an-hour; he popped up through the hatch to say goodnight.'

A quick flick back through recent events and I confirmed that he had—although I had completely forgotten about it.

'Is he asleep?'

'Just about. Sym's asleep by his feet, and Tigger's flat out on the other bunk. How do you feel?'

'Oh, I'm O.K.'

She looked up at the black sails and asked: 'How are we doing?'

'It's all right up here,' I said reassuringly, 'but I just went into the fo'c's'le to light the starb'd navigation lamp and the bilge sounded very noisy. Is it over the sealing?'

'Only a bit.' I had the impression that she was trying to reassure me.

'Are you O.K. now?' I asked anxiously.

'Yes, I'm fine; so is Kester. I think poor old Sym's the only one who's still suffering.' And then, equally anxiously: 'Do you feel tired?'

'No.' I examined myself mentally in some surprise—my reply had been automatic. 'No, I feel fine,' I added as I confirmed my state to myself. Well over twelve hours at the helm, I thought, and a long long night ahead . . . But I had to admit that I felt fine, just fine. Worried? Well, a little. Strained perhaps? My mind wandered back to the bilge—no, worried. Yes, I had to admit it: I was bloody worried about the leak. And then we would have to tack soon. Quickly I reminded myself that whatever happened I mustn't forget to release the rolling wang before we winded. Could Mollie handle the bowline in this wind? It would kick like the very devil! We'd ship some seas going about in this lot—would she be safe alone on the foredeck? On the foredeck . . . Hell! I still had the port lamp to light.

'Hang on there a minute,' I said, and I had a vague idea that I had interrupted her saying something. 'What did you say?'

'I said . . . Oh, it doesn't matter. What are you going to do?'

'Light the port lamp; won't be a minute. I'll fid the wheel, so don't worry about steering.'

I repeated my previous performance, and came on deck half-blinded by the match I had struck. The glow of the lamp reddened the hissing white horses to windward as I eased it into position; to leeward, the starboard lamp showed a mael-strom of green water racing astern. Hell to port, Old Man Neptune's green depths to starboard! And overhead the mighty spreet curved into the blackness like a gigantic bow, driving the arrow of the hull inshore towards destruction.

When I got back to the wheel Mollie said: 'I'll go and make a hot drink. What would you like: Oxo, tea or coffee?'

I looked towards the shore. A loom of light showed up almost dead ahead, and I knew that this would be Wells.

Distance off: the bugbear of coastal navigation! Oh, on well organised yachts the skipper would be taking three-point bearings and navigating like mad, so that he would know his margin of safety to the nearest (theoretical) few yards. But with us . . . The tide was ebbing; it was approaching midnight. Wells lay inland—up a creek which meandered across lord knows how many miles of sand and mud.

'Just a minute,' I said, 'let's have a look at the chart. Give me the torch, will you.

Mollie handed it up from the after cabin. I steadied the helm and fidded it before I switched on the bright light and turned to study the chart. One look would have to do; I couldn't afford to keep blinding myself.

'I reckon we're about here,' I mumbled, more to myself than to Mollie; 'just crossing Stiffkey Overfalls' (but I hadn't seen the Bridgirdle buoy—ah! unlit—no wonder). 'Now if we go right into Holkham Bay we'll miss some of the ebb for a while. That'll help a bit. When the soundings start dropping we'll wind. Then we'll be about three miles from Wells in a straight line.'

'Wait until we tack,' I told Mollie; 'then we can celebrate with a hot drink.'

'How long will that be?'

'About half-an-hour or so.'

At the end of my guessed time, we seemed to be no nearer our destination. The loom of Wells was still directly over our bow, but our position appeared to be exactly the same as before. Surely the blasted tide was not *that* powerful?

I fidded the helm, went to the weather leaning rail with the coiled lead-line, and cast it well forward. Two, three, four, five fathoms ran out, but no bottom. The line tailed away to wind-ward—phew! we were making a lot of leeway. I coiled it in and went back to the helm. In my mind, I could clearly picture the chart. Every part of the area in which we were sailing should have given a sounding of less—considerably less—than thirty feet. I fidded the helm again and tried a cast to leeward: forwards and outwards, to allow for the drift. This time I found the bottom at just over three fathoms. That was better! Well, we weren't in shallows yet.

But this diversion, which had taken some time, had brought me into closer proximity to the racing seas, and I began to wonder if it would not be wiser to tack now. Don't forget it's a dead lee-shore right ahead, I told myself, leave it too long, or miss a sounding like you did just now . . .

I watched the loom of the lights of Wells closely, but I still could not discern any gain. Better be safe than sorry, I thought. Much better. . . .

I peered into the dimly lit after cabin and saw that Mollie was sitting at the table knitting. 'Come on, darling,' I said quietly. 'We've got to go about.' I hated myself for having to drag her out, but there was absolutely no alternative. She put on her duffle coat and came up on deck, and whilst I waited for her night-sight to improve I explained exactly what I wanted her to do.

'Put the bowlin' *twice* around the shroud,' I said anxiously, 'and then pass the tail over the standing part and *hang on to it tightly with one hand*. It's going to kick like the devil in this wind, and if you lose it you won't be able to grab it again. With this sea running she might get into irons without the help of the bowlin', so for heaven's sake be ready for the sail flogging. And hang on to the middle shroud with your other hand—one hand for the ship, and the other for yourself. Remember?'

The oldest rule of the sea. She would remember that.

'Now, I've got to unrig the starboard rolling wang, and tie the end of the other to the rigging so that I can set it up as quickly as possible as soon as we're round,' I went on. 'Don't worry about the wheel—I'll set her on course. You just stay here for a minute.'

I made sure that *J & M* was on a steady course and then I ran forward and slacked off the rolling wang tackle, passed the wang back around the shrouds and made it fast to the foot of the spreet, unfastened the port rolling wang and passed it outside the shrouds, fastening the rope tail to the port forward shroud, nipped back to the tackle which I had left lying on the deck, overhauled it, and laid it ready for instant use on the port side deck, and then ran back to the wheel. She was still on course.

'Right-ho, darling. Now you go and rig the bowlin' and keep hanging on to it until I yell.'

Just in case—and I was beginning to shiver inside myself in awful anticipation of what was to come—just in case we shipped some heavy seas, I silently closed the sliding hatch over the after cabin. I had a sudden vision of Mollie and myself being swept away, leaving only Kester and Sym and Tigger down below—it had happened before, even in large square-rigged ships!—and then I was concentrating hard, peering to windward to try to pick the most advantageous moment to go about.

Mollie had disappeared into the blackness forward. Screened by the mainsail, with any possible silhouette blanketed by the foresail, it was impossible for me to see whether she had slipped overboard, or whether she was standing by and ready for action. And there was not very much to be seen to windward: a fleeting glimpse of white crests, an occasional slash of bloody water as we rolled upright and the navigation light cast a hellish glow, but nothing else. I couldn't pick a suitable lull from seeing, only from hearing and feeling for a break in the rhythm of the sea and the wind.

I guessed—right or wrong?—and began to luff. *J & M* seemed to falter in her stride with surprise. I gave her no chance to halt: I wound on the wheel furiously until a heavy *clunk* told me that it was fully over. I dropped the fid, clawed up the deck to windward, grabbed the capstan handle, felt it into position by touch, lifted the pawl, and lowered the port leeboard as rapidly as I could. Even as I worked, *J & M* came into wind.

The cacophony was terrifying! First, I heard the chain foresail sheet clank on deck, then it lifted and clanked again . . . overhead, faintly, I heard the rustle of the topsail as it lost its curve . . . then the mainsail flicked its tack. It was like an orchestra tuning-up. And then came the frustrated power! By my right knee, the iron traveller thundered across the main-horse, paused, and crashed back to starboard; the heavy, spiked, mainsheet block slammed ferociously against the mainhatch head and did its best to snap the mousing which held its hook to the traveller. Slashing and thrashing, with unseen ropes cracking like whips and with chains rattling as if the tormented ghosts of all creation had suddenly arrived, the sails and all their adornments began to flog. *J & M* shook to her keelson. It was appalling!

Keeping well clear of the berserk traveller and knobkerrie mainsheet block, I ran to starboard, fitted the winch handle, and cranked and cranked the starboard leeboard slowly upwards.

The mizzen flicked once, and then began to flog—we were nearly round.

Gasping for breath, hoping that the leeboard was fully up, I flung myself across to the wheel, lifted the fid, and raised my head to sense the wind direction. The mainsail was still flogging —but now it was more on the port side of the horse than the starboard.

Suddenly, the traveller gave a final *crash*, and stopped. We were round. I spun the wheel furiously, standing facing the spokes and using both hands. And as I worked, I roared out into the night:

'LET DRAW!'

For a moment, nothing . . . Then I heard the clank of the foresail sheet, the slither as it passed across the horse, and the final crash as the sail blew into position. Mollie was O.K. We were round safely. I fought with the helm almost happily as it

took me a good five minutes to steady her down on course
once more.

Mollie was soaked.

'Did we ship a sea?' I asked when she told me.

'Not one—three. It was awful. When we came up into wind
I was all ready and hanging on as you told me. When the wind
went out of the fores'l it gave one tremendous kick and tore the
bowlin' clean out of my hand. I was terrified! I grabbed out
and luckily I found it again. And then I tried to hang on to it.
But the shroud had gone slack and I was being dragged all over
the place—I simply *had* to use both hands to hang on to that
dam' bowlin'. That's when the first wave came over the port
bow. It must have sloshed into the fore hatch, because it
suddenly appeared from nowhere and went right over me.
Then the next wave broke right over the bows—I think. Any
rate I was up to my knees in water. I thought we were sinking.
And the noise was *awful*. I was wondering what to do when a
third wave went sort of woosh and sloshed into the fores'l—and
the bloody fores'l chucked the whole lot over me. Are we all
right?'

I told her, 'Yes, we got round O.K.'

'Will we have to make another tack tonight?'

I conjured up a reproduction of the chart. We probably had
two to three hours of ebb tide still to combat; on this losing
tack, with the tide against us, we should be driven back in the
general direction of the Burnham Flat buoy which we had
passed something like six or seven hours ago. The obvious
move would be to keep out of the tide as much as possible by
making short tacks along the coast, but I could not possibly
subject Mollie to that physical strain.

'We'll go offshore for a couple of hours, but we'll have to
make another tack before daylight,' I told her.

'I'll go down and get changed,' she said, 'and make a hot
drink. I wonder if all that noise woke Kester?'

She slid back the hatch and peered down.

'Well I'm damned—they haven't stirred.'

Where ignorance is bliss . . .

I kept her on deck until I had rigged the port rolling wang, and then she went below to change, and to brew-up and cut sandwiches. It took time, for which I was grateful: segmenting the night helped it to pass more quickly.

We were both worried and fearful about that second tack, but like all pre-imagined events it did not happen as supposed. I even made Mollie lash herself to the middle shroud! In the event, J & M winded smoothly—although still very noisily— and shipped no more than a little spray. Perhaps it was because we were in deeper water, or because wind and tide were now together; perhaps I was a bit luckier with a 'smooth'. We got round safely, that was all that mattered.

I persuaded Mollie, then, to try to get some sleep, and although she was reluctant to leave me alone she could see the sense of it. She left me some time after two, and I sat at the wheel of my ship and steered into the blackness of the night without any thoughts other than those necessary for the concentration of keeping to the best possible course—which is the only possible salvation for passing a long, lonely vigil and staying awake.

14. SECOND DAY

To sleep with your eyes open, to introvert, to withdraw into yourself so that external influences have no effect on your nervous system (apart from those to which you are attuned for survival reasons), is not easy. The faculty is natural, but man's incessant desire for security and safety has weakened the mental muscles of his survival instincts. He has lost a part of the art of living.

I sailed through the night at *J & M*'s wheel and steered a passable course to windward across the wild waters of the overland route. The blackness of the night was as unfathomable as my unbroken deep trance and I was undisturbed until dawn.

The transition from black to grey to colour, especially at sea, has delighted artists and poets since their first dawn. It has seldom cheered me, unless I have made a deliberate attempt to rise early in order to interpret the phenomenon. Dawn is an unwelcome early interruption to any all-night survival vigil, and it is only when the sun's rays warm a marble-cold body that it is worthwhile thawing back into life.

But the creeping lightening of the sky has a disturbing influence upon an open-eyed sleeper, and reluctantly I stirred and stretched as the early cold greyness brought my ship slowly back into vision. Presently, the sun tipped the horizon and silhouetted the black Himalayan-like waves in profile against its weak rays; then, almost at once, it slotted upwards into a bank of cloud, and the greyness returned—ugly in comparison. 'Come on sun,' I muttered; 'let's have some warmth.'

As the light increased I began to take an interest in where we were and how *J & M* had survived the night. Quietly I fidded the wheel and padded around the decks, alternating between

inspection and helm as was necessary to keep her on course. I
dowsed the navigation lights and stowed them away in the
fo'c's'le, I tidied those coils of halliards which had come adrift,
sorted out a tangle of warps which had been swept off the fore-
hatch into the scuppers by the seas which had come aboard
during the hectic inshore tack during the night. As I warmed to
my tasks, I shed the second sweater which I had worn since
sundown. Soon I had completed these chores, and I re-studied
the chart which had lain all night on the after-cabin roof, held
down by heavy shackles.

I reaffirmed that a flashing buoy which we had passed had
been Blakeney Overfalls—the exit (or entrance) to the overland route. We had gone between it and the shore, but I hadn't
known at what time, and it didn't really matter. I had known
where I was, and that was all that was necessary. Now we were
about two miles from the still-grey coastline, and the bob and
the wind told me that we were fighting a losing battle—in due
course we would have to tack offshore again. I guessed that the
black point far ahead was Cromer, and I remembered the battle
we had had getting round it when I had sailed *J & M* north
(the wind had headed us then, too!). Before sailing the route I
had thought that the coastline was quite smooth around the
forehead of Norfolk, but I had discovered that Cromer was a
Cape Horn of East Anglia: here the winds always headed you
whichever way you sailed!

With the coming of dawn, it seemed that the wind was losing
its punch. By six, I was quite sure that it was dropping: the
white horses no longer hissed in anger, the bob no longer
cracked viciously aloft, the sails were not straining at their
seams. The new topmast—by golly! I'd forgotten all about it—
the new topmast was only slightly bent. I went forward and
sighted up the spreet: the awe-inspiring bow of last night was
now just a reasonable curve. An hour later, the wind was no
more than Force 4.

The worse condition you can find for a barge is a bad seaway with little wind, and if the wind is against you, so much the
worse! The waves, thanks to last night's half-gale, continued

to hump towards the shore, lifting first the port chine so that
J & M was rolled to starboard, then shouldering under her flat
bottom until they could cock her starboard chine into the air.
With lessened wind pressure on her sails, *J & M* could not
combat their insistence on a reverse roll—so she went with
them. First to starboard, then a pause, then a sickening lurch to
windward which caused the spreet to snatch angrily at the confining rolling wang, and jerked all the tackles, blocks, chains
and halliards into a tinkling and crashing confusion of noise and
movement.

It woke Mollie and Kester just before eight.

'What on earth's all that row?' Kester wanted to know as he
poked his head through the hatch.

'The wind's dropping,' I told him briefly. 'We're going to
roll like hell now and there's not a thing I can do about it.'

Mollie looked out briefly, and I gave her the news. She said
nothing; she had suffered this before. She climbed down and
bundled bedraggled Sym on deck. He really did look unhappy.

'Tell you what, Kes,' I said. 'You'll find some short lengths of
wood in the starboard locker in the fo'c's'le. Dig out a couple
about two feet long and we'll prop open the entrance hatch so
that Sym can come on deck and go below when he wants to.'

Anything to cheer the dog up a bit!

I had breakfast at the wheel at nine, and the hot food and tea
cleansed the parrot's-cage mouth which I had developed during
the night through smoking my pipe. I felt fresh enough, but
the incessant rolling would soon have a depressive effect. I peed
over the side, lit my pipe, and watched the constantly slashing
sails—and worried.

We tacked offshore at nine-thirty. We were then about half-
a-mile off Sheringham, but I thought it would be best to make
sure of a good clearance around Cromer. Now we were
thrusting rather more directly into the seas, and although
the pitching stopped a lot of the way we did not roll nearly
so badly. We stood off to about three miles and winded
again. Back came the rolling!

By eleven, we were past Cromer and the wind had died to

Force 3. The early-morning clouds had dispersed, and the sun burnt down on us from a clear blue sky. Perhaps, I thought, it will heat up the land quick enough to give us a good sea breeze in the afternoon; but all it did was send the thermometer soaring, and give England the first real hot day of that summer. The wind, imperceptibly, kept on dying, and J & M with less and less wind resistance, kept on rolling.

Damage to a sailing ship from excessive strain generally results in breakage—like our topmast going over the side. Damage from chafe is much more insidious, and even more nerve-racking. Each lurching roll made me wince, and we were probably rolling at a rate of around three or four per minute. Say two hundred per hour. And every single back and forth movement jerked the shrouds, the stays, the wangs, the sails, the halliards . . . just imagine the sudden loads imposed by abruptly reversing the direction of travel of that five-ton mass of equipment which was balanced aloft!

I had set the staysail, of course. Anything to give some resistance to that dreadful snatch. And whilst the wind blew at Force 4, it helped a lot. But as the wind died to a breeze it became as useless as the other sails—all of them spilling the air far more often than they held it.

Around midday the topsail started to split. We were then about a mile offshore and still using the tide with some effect in spite of our slow sailing speed. The yellow beaches, the brown, grass-topped cliffs, moved very slowly astern although the panorama which unfolded showed little change since the whole coastline was largely characterless. Yellow beaches, mostly deserted, and brown, grass-topped cliffs which occasionally grew a rash of caravans. I had no doubt that many a binocular would be in use from such vantage points: 'Cor, look, dad, there's a big sailing boat.' And dad would seize his latest 20 × 60 purchase and try to hold us steady in its quivering bloomed lens. 'Lucky sods,' he would say. 'Now if I had a good win on the Pools . . .' And J & M would look photogenically glorious as she wallowed across the blue, sunny waters.

Slowly we were driven inshore by the combination of seas

and wind: too much of one, too little of the other. By one o'clock we were rolling so badly that occasionally we were lipping a wave-top over the rails—either to weather or lee-ward. We had rolled badly before, but I had never seen any-thing as bad as this. I had to anchor—this I knew—but as long as we had way, and the tide helped us, I intended to keep her going. Go on, you bitch; keep going! She slashed and rattled in a fury of ineffectual rolling movement—but she kept going all the same. And I worried every inch of the way with her.

I had no idea of what else had happened that morning. Mollie brewed hot drinks which I sipped, and Kester asked questions which possibly I answered. I doubt if I was com-municative. Sym added a minor worry which nagged in the back of my mind: he still hadn't 'gone'; he prowled the decks seeking a suitable spot, but he was being as difficult as a recruit on his first medical parade! I could not believe that his bladder or bowels would burst, but it was still a worry to add to the list. Whine you may, I thought, but go you must. It was a weak pun. Both Sym and *J & M* were protesting about 'going.' Oh, if only I could do something to stop one and start the other. That was an even worse joke!

Towards the end of that terrible period—and she had been rolling badly for at least six hours—I edged abruptly ashore. The time was two o'clock, the breeze so fitful that it would barely have moved us over calm waters; only the seas continued to roll towards the yellow beaches, where they burst to a thunderous climax which would have delighted any surfing addict.

Three hundred yards from the beach off Happisburgh (pronounced Haisbra) I dropped anchor in two fathoms—giving her only five fathoms of chain because I doubted my strength to recover more than this if the wind suddenly increased. I lowered the staysail and foresail and set up both wangs as tightly as I could. I was not prepared to waste time or effort on the other sails: I rucked the topsail, part-brailed the main, and left the mizzen set. And then for fifteen glorious minutes I lay in the gentle folds of the white staysail and shut my eyes and ears to the tumult which had gone on for such a long long time. Fifteen minutes—it wasn't much—but it helped. *J & M*, sensibly, swung her stern towards the shore, and began to pitch more than she rolled. The hot sun was deliciously enervating: if only I could lay and soak and forget everything. . . . But the demands of my ship had still to be met —there was no time for dozing. The inanimate forced the pace on the animate. Wearily, I went below.

Take the living space in your house or bungalow, or your best front room, and fill it with *salt* water to a depth of nine inches. Better still, to ensure absolute accuracy with this simile, make it fifteen inches deep, because *J & M*'s frames under the sealing were eight inches wide by six inches thick, and there were nine inches of water *over* the sealing. Now rock your room, or house, viciously, through a ninety degree arc at the rate of four times per minute for six hours. From time to time, add coal dust, mildewed grain, sand, rust, Thames mud, brick dust, tar, and almost anything else which is either dirty or smelly. It makes an evil cocktail.

Mollie, the previous evening, with Kester's help, had got up all the carpets. Now I learned for the first time why they had been so long down below. Almost everything which could be damaged by the filthy bilge had been stacked on tables or chairs or in our bedroom under the fore-hatch which was still dry (thanks to *J & M* being trimmed six inches by the stern). But they couldn't move everything. My library, on shelves under the decks in the saloon, three feet above the sealing, had acted as breakwaters to the surge of water every time we rolled. All were sodden. The Esse-Dura stove sat on its brick hearth like a lighthouse on a rock—and as storm-washed! A large wooden trunk, containing notes and priceless flying photographs which I had taken during the war, had sunk at its usual stowage position under the companion-way—its entire contents probably ruined. Mollie's spotless galley was a desperate chaos of salvaged utensils and food—and filth.

And even now, as *J & M* pitched and rolled in the oily seaway, the bilge sloshed and battered at the confining walls of

our home. It was useless to say anything. I went wearily on deck to start up the sludge pump, which had for so long obstructed my every movement on the port quarter deck.

It started easily enough—first go, in fact. I slid the heavy hose into the cabin where, directly under the sliding hatch, the floorboards could be lifted to get at the 4-inch wooden peg which was J & M's bilge-plug. Even here, in spite of the raised sole, the water was only an inch or so short of the floorboards. The engine ran for perhaps three minutes . . . then it spluttered . . . then it stopped! The jet of black water which had been shooting gloriously out of the delivery hose over the side died slowly to a few drips. I cursed, cranked the handle, and the four-stroke started again quite easily—but within a couple of minutes it spluttered again to a standstill.

I am no mechanic, but I knew what this meant: water in the system. I would have to drain the tank, the carburettor and the fuel pipes. I started it again, and went unwillingly to the fo'c's'le to try to find some spanners which might fit.

Because my ship had never had to rely on any form of mechanical drive, my collection of spanners could hardly be described as complete. I had some heavy stuff for the rigging, and a King Dick and a small shifter, and I had a wide range of rusty spanners and box-spanners which I had · found and collected over the years—and two or three ring spanners, too. But no matter what I tried, I did not have any which could reach the bolts that held the one gallon petrol tank in place on the pump. And I knew it would be in the tank that I would find the water droplets which were causing all the trouble.

Out of all the jobs which I have tackled, tinkering with engines is the one I loathe most. I was scarcely in the right mood to consider this one. Desperate measures occurred to me, but I rejected them all on the grounds that I would find it impossible to overcome the lethargy which worry, lack of sleep, constant movement, and the heat of the sun were imposing on me. We were still in the open sea; as far as I could see, I would have to spend another night at the helm; it seemed to me that this battle could go on and on and on. . . .

So I cranked the engine into life again, and when it stopped I waited a minute and cranked it up again . . . and again . . . and again. . . . It was not the best solution, but it was all I could manage. I had no rest. . . . Presently, it became more and more difficult to re-start the engine. . . . In due course it flatly refused to start any more. But by then it had been running on and off for two hours, and it had reduced the bilge to a 3-inch deep puddle at the after end of the saloon around the fireplace. There was, of course, still all the water *under* the sealing!

Mollie insisted then that I ate, and somehow from the soggy mess in her galley she contrived to heat up a bowl of soup. In spite of the sun, I enjoyed this 'lunch'. I was amazed to discover, when I finished, that it was really tea-time.

Apart from my cursory look at the flood, I had not been below again. Mollie and Kester had had some food in the after cabin soon after we anchored, but I had wanted to get the pump going before I ate. I had my soup on deck. I would not relax below in the comfort of the after cabin in case I developed a physical and psychological revulsion to recommencing the ordeal; I had seen it happen before, and I did not want it to happen to me.

There was no time for rest. I dismantled the pump hose and stowed it back on deck, replacing the floorboards and the ladder. I went slowly around the decks and rigging, re-lashing this, tightening that, checking and re-checking everything. I climbed aloft and tried to find the ripped seam in the topsail, but it was lost in the loose but heavy folds. I checked over the gear whilst I was up there, and found that it was all as it should be.

With the sun beating down so intensely that my already-brown body was reddening, it seemed ridiculous to suppose that the wind would return in the same strength as the previous night. There were no mare's-tails reminders in the clear blue sky, and even the rollers were becoming subdued as the heat-wave beat upon them—the sun seemed to be that hot! I wore only shorts, and the sweat from my exertions ran down my body in rivulets. Somehow it never occurred to me to waste my energies by going in for a swim.

So for about an hour and a half after eating I did what I could
do for my ship, and mentally involved myself into the next
night's battle by studying the chart from time to time. Everything depended on the wind direction and strength. I waited
for it to come.

Mollie was doing things below—I presumed that she was
looking after her section of the ship with the same concentration as my part demanded. Kester, knowing my propensity for
retiring into myself with my problems, played on deck in
happy loneliness. Sym prowled, or slumped, panting, on a
shady portion of deck—only to scrabble upright and prowl
again; he was not happy. Tigger condescended to have a look
around, and then retired to his favourite shelter under the
steering-box by the taffrail where he slept peacefully through
most of the afternoon. Thus, each of us did what our own
consciences dictated, and it would seem that Kester and Tigger
had the least to worry about and Sym the most. I doubt if there
was very much difference between Mollie's problems and
mine—and we both thought of each other's worries too. But
it would have been as pointless to talk about them as it was to
attempt to persuade Sym to 'go' on deck. I even tried urinating
by the mast as an encouragement, but he failed to understand—
dogs are as dim-witted as horses, and can never hope to achieve
the absolutely independent intelligence of cats. I paused
occasionally in my worried meanderings: kids and cats—they
have a pretty good time on the whole. And then a fresh worry
would occur to me and I would forget all about their innocent
pleasures in a welter of re-revised pros and cons. It was all very
silly, really, but it's the way we're made.

The first whisper of breeze came at five-thirty. A few cat's-
paws scattered across the oily rollers and brushed against our
heated bodies. The bob stirred, squeaked and fluttered the
swallow-tails; the mainsail and mizzen rustled gently. Tentatively, the breeze fanned around from all directions; a puff
from the north-east, a whisper from the south-east. . . . (No, no.
Not a south-easterly, *please*.) Then, suddenly, it came to a
decision, and whispered a promise from the east—just enough

ME

to head us once more so that we would still have a flog dead to windward.

Although the hour was later, I had a feeling that we would be getting a repetition of the previous afternoon's breeze-up, and I had a sudden horror of being caught on this lee shore, unable to get our anchor.

'Come on,' I said to Kester. 'We've got to get out of here.'

I sheeted out the main, and hoisted the topsail. Then, up foresail, shove it on the bowline, and ship winch handles. And there we were sailing away. The anchor must have been just lying on the bottom without digging in. Hurriedly I called to Mollie to give Kester a hand to crank up the last of the anchor chain, whilst I eased the wangs, steered, and reapplied myself to the task of sailing southwards.

The topsail did not look very healthy. One seam near the leech had ripped its stitches and unzipped as far as a cross-seam in the belly. The tear had then crossed the cloth and continued to rip a little way both up and down the next seam. A slash of blue sky showed through the gap. If it went much further the topsail would undoubtedly collapse. Another worry!

I soon discovered that although I could not claw off the shore very much, *J & M* could just about gain precious yards to windward if I concentrated at the job. I knew that the staysail would have helped, but I felt sure that the wind would keep increasing. It did. By seven it was blowing at a steady Force 6 as before.

For a time, the wind seemed to flatten the last of those rollers which had caused us so much worry and damage. But relentlessly the seas began to build up once more: first to choppyness, then to lippy waves and the first white horses. . . . As evening descended, the wind chilled; soon the beaches were deserted. The tunnel of another long night loomed ahead. . . .

As we battled against the last of the ebb, and the sun sank behind the low cliffs of the lonely Norfolk beaches, I tried to make up my mind as to whether I should tack offshore or continue on our present course crawling along the shore. Here, we were out of the main current; a tack offshore would lose considerable ground with the adverse wind slant and current.

If I waited until the tide turned, we would be inside the jaws of the various sand and shingle banks, which open up as a ship approaches Yarmouth Roads from the north. I knew that the correct manœuvre should be to get out into the main channel and away from the unlit dangers which lay ahead of us, but I could not bring myself to give up a lot of the ground which we had gained through hanging on when the rolling was at its worst.

No! We would hang on—and keep going. But this time we were heading directly into a trap from which there could be no possible escape once we were committed. In all fairness to Mollie and Kester, I showed them what I intended to do whilst there was still a chance to take the alternative route. I spread the new chart on the after coachroof, pinned it down with the shackles, and pointed out the possibilities.

'We can't gain any more ground to wind'ard than we're making now,' I explained, 'and so we must go through this gap here—Hemsby Hole. It's unlit. What we *should* do is make a board two or three miles offshore and pick up the Cockle light-buoys in the main channel, but if we do that we'll waste a lot of time and lose a good deal of ground. Shall we keep on this tack —in which case we should be inside the sheltered Yarmouth Roads by about eleven; or shall we go offshore, lose ground, but take the safer route—and get inside the Roads say a couple of hours later?'

Kester said: 'Let's go inshore. I can stay up and keep a look-out for you.'

Mollie said: 'That inshore route looks very dangerous. Can you find your way in the dark?'

I said: 'The wind's about Force 6 now. It may increase when it gets dark. I don't want you to have another battle like you had last night, and I reckon the seas will be pretty bad out in the Cockle Gat. As far as I'm concerned I think that sheltered water for the night is worth the risk!'

Both Mollie and I were in complete agreement on this point; Kester was thrilled with the thought of the adventure.

Reluctantly I went back to the wheel, lifted the fid, and steered a course towards potential suicide. . . .

15. SECOND NIGHT

J & M lumbered southwards against the last of the ebb, just about beating the tide. In the fading light I felt the usual anxieties. After the heat of the day, the deepening haze on the horizon and the white-crested grey seas looked bleak and threatening, and under our lee the rounded backs of the breakers thundered monotonously on the deserted beaches.

I was having to keep *J & M* as close-hauled as possible in order to avoid making another tack. It was difficult to accomplish, and foolish to attempt. Every so often I would not be quick enough on the helm, and she would gripe up over the shoulder of a wave towards the wind. The luff of the topsail would give me the first warning: it would begin to belly just above the hounds; then the foresail would lose the full weight of the wind from its ample curves, and the chain sheet would clank limply on deck. Wearily I would have to stand up from my seat on the coachroof in order to give her lee helm quickly. The bows would lift to the next wave, drop into the next trough, and rise again to the following crest before they would begin to swing downwind. During those seconds, if I had not checked the swing quick enough, sometimes the mainsail would lift and begin to shake.

I grumbled within myself at the lousy luck which we had had with the wind on this passage. As I worked continually at the helm—up, down, up, down, like a bloody yo-yo—I went back over the course and realised that not once, not bloody once, had we really found a slant. When we had rounded the bend of the river off Hull I thought we would be O.K.—but we had been forced to tack. When we passed Donna Nook, I thought I had freed the wind—but now I realised that instinctively I had kept her as close-hauled as possible in an attempt to clear Blakeney Point. All the way I had been forced to nurse my ship along as close to the wind as she could be persuaded to go, and yet I was very aware of the fact that barges do not like being pinched to windward. As a result, we had made poor time—and yet I couldn't help wondering if we would have come even this far if I had not kept her at it, on and on and bloody on!

Now, as I eased her along the very fringe of the surf, with darkness imperceptibly eliminating visual guides, I had committed myself to clawing to windward into an unlit bottle-neck trap. There would be no second chance here: no hope of tacking with the barely covered bank closing in to port and pinning us on the lee shore, no hope of wearing ship by gybing because we were too close to the beaches. If the wind altered half a point to the south—just half a point, that's all it needed—we were done for; I could only wind, and hope that she would be able to turn and run out of the enfolding walls of the bottle-neck. But in the darkness how could we hope to survive such a manœuvre? And even if we did, we would lose the protection of the Scroby Sands and have to battle to windward in unprotected seas for another night. I still felt sure I had done the right thing, but I also knew the terrible risk I was taking.

Earlier, shortly after we had left Happisburgh, I had asked Kester to fill and trim the port and starboard navigation lamps. Before he went to bed (and how he objected!) he had lit them for me, and I had made two hurried trips from the wheel to sling them on the boards. I did not bother about a stern-light; like the night before, we were not sailing in any shipping lanes.

So Kester was in bed and asleep as the crisis approached.

Mollie stood by—as she had done last night. I could guess her anxiety, although I doubted if she could possibly be any more worried than I.

Just before the blackness of night closed in I had a last look at the bendy topmast and the rip in the topsail, now about six foot in overall length. I looked—but that was all I could do. The wind was a steady Force 6, the seas steep and foam-flecked, the night sky clear but without a moon, and the tide had turned in our favour and was making strongly.

I had one guide—just one! The chart showed a coastguard lookout at East Caister. I assumed that in such an important position as the north end of the Yarmouth Roads this post would always be manned. I assumed—I didn't know. Just off the beach at this point the Hemsby Hole Gap was at its narrowest, the off-lying Caister Shoal almost meeting the shore. If the coastguard post was manned it would be lit. Spot the light, judge distance off, and we'd be through The Gap. . . . There were an awful lot of 'ifs'.

We were now well into Hemsby Hole and the seas were not nearly so vicious, thanks to some protection from the Cockle Bank.

Distance off! That's what mattered. I could see from the chart that the nearer I sailed to the shore the less chance there would be of touching on any of the shallower portions of the Cockle or the Caister. I kept *J & M* as close to the breakers as I dared. The tide's making, I told myself, there'll be plenty of water. With about a mile and a half to go I snatched one last look at the dew-limp chart on which this distance was represented by a meagre three-quarters of an inch; then, with the details and soundings firmly imprinted on my mind, I switched off the torch and concentrated entirely on the task of popping *J & M* out through the neck of the bottle.

When my eyes had blinked away the brightness of the torch light, I fidded the wheel and peered round the straining mainsail. There *was* a light on the shore—entirely separate from the conglomeration of street, house and car lights which were beginning to prick up through the general glow which was Great Yarmouth. At that distance it was a mere dot, but it was exactly where I had expected to see it and therefore it *must* be the right one. I went hurriedly back to the wheel and checked that we were still as close-hauled as possible.

Gradually, and so imperceptibly that I did not appreciate the significance, I heard a steadily increasing muted roar. At first, it seemed to come from all around, but as we drove onwards into the blackness I isolated its source to an area forward of the port beam. But still I could not analyse the sound.

Every few minutes, I fidded the wheel and peered to starboard at my guiding light. Until it was proved otherwise I intended to hang on to this only straw. There was no other guidance, the shoreline now having completely disappeared in the night. I judged our angle to the light, allowing for leeway, and pressed on. I didn't do much, really, since the route which we followed was identical with the closest course I could nurse *J & M* into the half-gale.

The drive of the wind in the sails and rigging, plus the gurgle of captured water behind the leeboard, and the general hiss of the seas from our passage through them, made it impossible for me to locate exactly the direction and character of that muted roar. Once again I fidded the wheel: this time to go forward—right up by the stayfall blocks. Now there was only the slosh of the bow-wave; now I could hear what was happening.

In the blackness around me the tide was flowing strongly—racing southwards. You cannot see tidal direction, even in daylight, unless there is a stationary object to oppose the movement; nor, in daylight, can you generally *hear* the tide. But this night I heard it. The full vigour of the flood was sluicing across the banks which surrounded us—some of sand, some of shingle. To windward the seas were pounding against the Cockle and the Caister Shoal. Ahead, to windward and to leeward, the banks must be all shingle for it was from this area that the noise was loudest. It was awe-inspiring. I was very afraid.

There was no time now to take soundings, no hope of restudying the chart; nothing left but to go with the mill-race and stay at the helm and do my best to aim my ship towards that narrow gap in the roaring shingle.

We were getting very close to the guiding light. It was no longer just a round blob of brightness—now it had become square and assumed an identity. Distance off! I knew that the shingle bank extended outwards from the Coastguard lookout —but how far? I began to edge *J & M* more and more into wind. Then I had an idea. Navigate by sound!

I fidded the wheel again and ran forward. The roar was no longer muted. A million tons of shingle was being scoured into movement by tide and breakers, and we were very nearly in the middle of it. To port was a seething whiteness of turmoil where the seas were disturbed into chaos by the shallowness of the water—this was the main source of the noise. To starboard, a line of more regular surf indicated the position of the Coast-guard's shingle beach. And further to starboard—now almost level with us—the yellow light from their window silhouetted two figures who seemed to be standing and peering outwards. . . . Had they seen our lights?

These impressions were fleeting and fractional snippets of information which my mind translated into joyous relief even as I ran back to the wheel: *J & M* had gone through the bottle-neck, slap-bang-wallop in the centre! From those few precious seconds spent forward I judged that we had gone through a gap no wider than a hundred to a hundred-and-fifty yards, if the distance between the two white masses of surf had indicated the channel—which they must have done. We were through! We were bloody through! Talk about shoving a camel through the eye of a needle; what about poking a barge out through the neck of a bottle?

I seized the top spokes of the wheel and eased *J & M* gently on her way for another fifteen minutes or so. The roar of the undertow died behind us. To starboard, the lights of Great Yarmouth seafront took form; to port, the winking buoys of Yarmouth Roads guaranteed navigational security for the rest of the night. Through Hemsby Hole Gap, and with adequate water under our lee for the first time since before we had anchored off Happisburgh, I fidded the wheel and peered into the after cabin to pass the glad tidings to Mollie.

Kester was fast asleep in the starboard bunk, with Tigger curled up (and no doubt purring gently) at his midriff. Sym occupied the port bunk, and slumbered—though uneasily—with Mollie's hand on his head to soothe away his fears. And Mollie slept too, part-sitting on the hard wooden bench, part-leaning on Sym's rump as she had reached out to stroke him.

The Aladdin lamp was turned down to a dim glow. After the stresses of the past few hours I felt very emotional at that moment.

Minutes later, Mollie put her head out of the hatch. 'Are we through?' she asked quietly.

'I thought you were asleep,' I said. 'I just had a look—'

'I know. I heard you. I just wanted a minute to myself. We're through, aren't we?'

'Yes,' I said, 'we're through.'

There was a brief pause.

'I'll go and make you a hot drink,' she said. 'I expect you could do with one.'

With the terrors of shooting The Gap behind us, only the monotony of the long night was left. Compared with the open sea, the Yarmouth Roads were a quiet lagoon, and in spite of the strength of the wind it would be very nearly a joy-ride.

After we had finished our drinks I persuaded Mollie to turn in, and although she was reluctant to leave me, eventually she went below. She wanted me to anchor in the Roads, or try to get into the Yare—which is Great Yarmouth's harbour. I would not anchor because I doubted our ability to crank up twenty fathoms or so of chain, and I would not attempt the harbour entrance in this wind because I knew that we were too short-handed to tackle a gybe round the notorious right-angled Brush Bend just inside.

'I'm O.K.,' I told her. 'I can keep going for ages yet. You try and get some sleep though—there's absolutely nothing you can do on deck.'

For the first time on the passage I was able to relax a little at the wheel. Since passing through The Gap, we had actually freed our wind, so that it was very nearly on our port beam. I eased the wangs and mainsheet slightly, reset-up the starboard rolling wang, and almost revelled in my freedom from the laborious concentration of keeping my ship hanging on to a dead-to-windward course.

Whether it was this easier reach, or because the worries of the open sea and Hemsby Hole Gap were over, I was not sure, but the wind strength certainly seemed to have decreased. Two hours after entering Yarmouth Roads I was sure it had, because by then it was no more than Force 4. Now that we were in sheltered waters (sheltered when compared with what we had been through), it would not have mattered if the wind had continued to blow hard all night—it could only have helped us on our way more quickly. Instead it died very slowly, so that when the tide turned it was barely strong enough to keep us going over the powerful ebb which sweeps northwards between the outlying banks and the shore. By then we had just passed Lowestoft, no more than half-a-mile out, passing directly over the treacherous Newcombe Bank.

It is, of course, perfectly safe to cross the Newcombe at the top of the tide; if the weather is fair, a light barge can cross at low water. But this bank can be very dangerous in an onshore blow, and as I was now over the middle of it and barely stemming the ebb tide I began a new worry which lasted the rest of the night.

In the distance, I could see the flash of Southwold lighthouse. We were so close inshore that I was in the red sector of the light ('You are standing into danger'), but this I knew already so I wasn't bothered about it. What did worry me was that the wind might drop further and force me to anchor on the shoals, since I could not bear to think of drifting astern and losing ground; neither would I like to make the decision of anchoring in that dangerous position. As long as we could keep going. . . .

Instead of nursing *J & M* to windward all night, I spent the hours worrying her along foot by foot, yard by yard. . . . It was just as much a strain as the previous night—worse, in fact, because the hours dragged by as slowly as my ship gained ground.

So all that night I watched the almost stationary shoreline. The harbour lights of Lowestoft passed imperceptibly astern, but the street lights to the south of the harbour stayed with me. And ahead, off our starboard bow, the red light from Southwold rotated its repeated warning.

Once again I hunched myself into introspection in an attempt to make the night pass more quickly. But this time I was not entirely able to assume the trance-like state which is very nearly as good as a deep sleep. Perhaps the Hemsby Hole incident had disturbed me more than usual—certainly I continued to think about the narrowness of our escape, instead of automatically obliterating the unpleasant past which is the only possible survival tactic during any adventure. Perhaps the ever present image of the *Flying Dutchman* began to brew fanciful notions to a mind which was already overtired by worry, but had to cope with a body which ached from inactivity and yet protested violently whenever physical action was required of it: my bottom was numb from constant sitting, my legs were weary from constant standing, my arms and shoulders could barely heave and shove the spokes of the wheel, back and forth, forth and back. . . . The moon rose and tipped the black waters with silver. . . . Later I spotted one of the black conical Barnard buoys silhouetted against the light. . . . We were clear of the Newcombe!

Later still, I distinctly saw somebody climb over the port bow—presumably up the anchor. I was a little surprised about this, and I did not immediately go forward to greet him because I could not make up my mind as to whether it was a line fisherman whom we had run down, or a sailing dinghy which had capsized. Then I got a notion that it must be Sinbad, and I fidded the wheel a little nervously and went forward to where he was standing by the bitts. As I walked forward, wondering whether to start off with a simple 'Good Evening', I saw that he was climbing back over the bow. By the time I had ducked past the creaking shrouds and run to the stem he had disappeared. I searched the blackness to leeward, and the silvery seas to windward, but there was no sign of him. I was very puzzled. Well, if he didn't want to stay and say hello. . . . I shrugged my shoulders and went back to the wheel. I was a bit peeved. Making use of *J & M* like that, and not a bloody word. . . .

The sails rustled quietly and the rigging creaked, the lee-board bumped occasionally as a heavier swell made *J & M* lurch out of rhythm. The peace of the night was absolute, the monotony of the watch complete. But we kept going on and on into the blackness ahead.

It seemed to me that my self-imposed task was as ridiculous as any other struggle to get somewhere. The similarity of battling against odds was as identical during a lifetime as it was on this passage. As soon as one obstacle is overcome, the next turns up—each causing a new worry and thereby increasing the overall strain. But what was the point of it all? In our case, we had to go somewhere, or lose out on the way—but if we arrived safely, what then? In a lifetime of striving to get somewhere, what did one find at the end of the voyage? Just death—the same for everybody. Only the immortality of the *Flying Dutchman* could be worse.

I was no longer angry with whoever had come on board, because I knew now why they had come. 'You're over the Newcombe,' was the message. 'You're safe now. Drop anchor here. Rest.' But my answer had winged out long before I understood the implications: 'We cannot stop. It is not in our nature to give up. We must go on.' Regretfully he had left, and his final whisper had come softly through the darkness to blend with all the other sounds of my ship in the night: 'Go, then, go. But there will be no peace . . . no peace until death. . . .'

Southwold lighthouse continued to rotate its red warning: 'You are standing into danger. You are standing into danger.'

It was the strangest night vigil I have ever kept, from its Valkyrie-like terrors as we stormed into Hemsby Hole to its Midsummer Night's Dream ending. How much had I contributed to the salvation of my ship? I brooded in solitude. . . .

Still later, came the dawn.

16. THIRD DAY

The sun rose over a clear horizon, and my third day at the helm began. I rejoiced only at the elimination of that cursed red light; the glory of the birth of a perfect summer's day was almost completely lost on me. Of what possible use was it when the wind was no more than Force 3, and the tide was ebbing?

J & M's decks were wet with dew, and the rigging sparkled diamonds, but I could only wriggle my numb backside on the flattened, damp cushion and hope that Mollie would soon wake up and make some tea.

To leeward, Southwold gleamed prettily in the sunlight, the white buildings and emerald greensward stark against the blue sky. We were about a mile offshore, and from here the place looked like a beautifully coloured photograph. 'Come to Dozey Southwold where Summer is as Summers were; Come and Play Bowls on the Greensward, Where the Guns will Protect You and You Will Remember Drake.' But wasn't that Plymouth? Anyway, the milk bottles would be rattling along those silent streets, and the bees would be starting up engines for another day's buzz around, and soon people would be getting up and turning on wireless sets and making turmoil and absolutely ruining the peace as they always did. But none of them, and nobody else in the world, could sit here, in charge of their own 115-ton sailing ship, and know what Southwold looked like first thing on that particular morning. . . .

I wished I was ashore, asleep between clean sheets . . . clean sheets. . . .

I had the most appalling hangover, and a mouth like a navvy's armpit. I had not rested with the same fortitude that I had managed to achieve the night before. Why? I had had fewer worries. No: there had been the dying wind and the Newcombe! But that was nothing after the terrors of Hemsby Hole the previous night—or was it last night? How long *had* we been under way? We'd started on the Wednesday—yes, market-boat day. Well, what was today? The first night was going across the Wash, the second night was off Sheringham, the third night was Hemsby Hole, and last night we were off Lowestoft. . . . So today's Sunday. No wonder Southwold's so ruddy peaceful. How long had I been at the helm then? Wednesday from eight to Thursday at eight: twenty-four hours. Thursday to Friday: forty-eight hours. Friday to Saturday . . . Three fours are twelve: two, carry one; three twos are six—that's seventy-two hours! Seventy-two up to this morning at eight? No, that's wrong. Start again: Wednesday to Thursday is one day, and Thursday to Friday—But we left on a Friday, not a bloody Wednesday. . . . So what was today? It must be Monday—no, Tuesday. But it couldn't be. . . .

The sun warmed me gently, and *J & M* pitched very lazily over the blue, dancing seas.

'The wind was rising easterly, the morning skies were blue.' I recited, 'the straits before us opened wide and free. We looked towards the Admiral where high the Peter flew, and all our hearts were dancing like the sea. . . .'

We sang it at school. What was it called? 'The Old Superb', that's it!

'Round the world if need be, and round the world again, with a lame duck lag, lag, lagging all the way!

'The Old Superb was barnacled, and green as grass below; her sticks were only fit for stirring grog. . . .'

Well that was a damn silly thing to do. Think of the difficulties of getting the sticks out of her just to stir grog! Now what was the method? You made sheerlegs of the topsail yards and you set up a fivefold tackle—or was it a fourfold? . . . How had I set up *J & M*'s mast? I'd got it alongside by floating it, but it had been a problem heaving it up over the side because the hounds had jammed against the 'wale. . . .

Mollie said: 'Are you asleep?'

I answered instantly: 'Of course not.' And then: 'What's the time?'

'Just after seven-thirty.'

We were still on course, reaching across the easterly breeze against the tide. Southwold was still to starboard, distance one mile. What time was dawn? Four?

It had been a queer night.

'Did the Benzedrine help?' Mollie asked.

'What Ben—' Then I remembered. Of course, when we had the hot drinks last night Mollie had suggested that a Benzedrine might help me to stay awake. . . .

'I don't think it made much difference,' I told her. 'Probably helped a bit, I suppose.'

I said no more. I had doubted at the time the advisability of my taking a drug. In my Air Force days, I flatly refused any injections or drugs unless absolutely necessary, and I even regarded a common-or-garden Aspirin in the same light. Like a fool, I had let Mollie persuade me into taking one, just one, Benzedrine. I felt we had had a very narrow escape. That figure who had come aboard last night. . . . And this morning. . . . Bloody drugs! And yet the man and the voice had seemed so real. . . .

'How about some breakfast?' I said to Mollie. 'I'm starving. Is Kester up?'

'Yes, I'm here,' Kes said, squirming up the ladder alongside Mollie. 'Coo! What a smashing morning. Was it all right last night?'

'Yes, it was all O.K.' I assured him.

It was—now.

The sun dried the decks; I ate a good breakfast, then Mollie brought up a bowl of hot water and I washed and shaved at the wheel. I felt better—much, much better—but a great weariness was now creeping over me so that all I really wanted to do was sleep . . . sleep. . . .

By ten we were no more than three or four miles further on our way. Southwold was still only just behind us. We would make no real progress until the tide turned.

At mid-day we were off Sizewell. It was a pitiful crawl.

I did not expect a wind of any strength in that heatwave. The hot sun beat down throughout the morning as we crept slowly over the tide, and the only event of importance was that Sym finally decided to 'go'. He 'went' in profusion on the neatly coiled starboard wang fall and I was as relieved as he undoubtedly was, although it meant trailing the rope in the water for a couple of hours, and several buckets of water on the deck!

The easterly breeze stayed reasonably constant, occasionally puffing up to Force 4 for a few minutes, but mostly whispering gently around us at Force 3. I hoisted the staysail immediately after washing and shaving—which gave me the moral boost to tackle the job. Apart from that brief expenditure of energy, I relapsed once again at the helm and brooded the hours away in silent contenplation of nothing—except to get *J & M* into some haven before darkness descended for a third night at sea.

We had a sandwich lunch at around one—all of us sitting around the wheel, including Sym (waiting for tit-bits) and Tigger (just waiting, as cats sometimes do), and helping ourselves to the food which Mollie had laid out so neatly on a tray. A picnic on deck. Off our starboard bow, only a couple of miles or so away, Orfordness headland and white lighthouse were in brilliant contrast against the blue seas and sky. The tide was on the turn. We'd be able to make Harwich Harbour that afternoon even if the wind died away to nothing. I was almost happy. My defences were down. Two or three hours and we would be anchored, and this ordeal would be a memory.

The gods laughed. . . .

The wind came literally out of the blue. If I had not been so tired, so lethargic, so confident that we were nearly there, I would have noted the warnings in the sky: the yellow haze to windward, the stark brilliance of buildings against the sky, the high cirrus. But I had not noticed, and I had not bothered to notice: I had started to spend my winnings before I received them.

The only warning which finally registered was when the breeze suddenly faded away. *J & M* rolled sluggishly in the oily calm, and for the first time that morning the sails slatted and the gear tinkled. I shivered up my spine as icy premonition stung me into action. I jumped to my feet and looked quickly astern. Then, and only then, did I see what was coming—but by then it was almost too late.

The wind had backed four points. Almost dead astern it was coming at us like an express train, the power and speed of its approach showing clearly on the smooth lumps of the morning's peaceful seaway. Already in the distance I could see white horses and the return of a Himalayan-strewn horizon.

'Get the grub down below,' I shouted to Kester.

He scrambled down the hatch and Mollie handed the tray down to him.

'We must get the stays'l off at once,' I told her urgently. 'You go and release the halliard with a run. I'll come and smother it.'

She hurried forward, but not quick enough. The first puffs of wind arrived, and then it was blowing a good Force 5 within seconds.

'Hurry!' I bawled. 'Let the halliard go!'

But even as I shouted J & M began to move to the wind pressure: she could not gather way quick enough, so she began to nose her bows downwards as the colossal leverage of all her sails pressed her forward. As she dived, the rudder lost its grip on the water. Simultaneously I heard a Niagara-like roar of water, and realised that this was our bilge rushing forward with the angle of the ship.

Mollie obeyed instructions and released the halliard. The staysail, with the pressure of the wind in it, slid barely a third of the way down the topmast forestay—and stuck. Regardless of gybing or broaching-to risks (for the biggest immediate danger was the staysail) I fidded the wheel and rushed forward. Within seconds I was handing the slashing, wild, almost uncontrollable white sail—standing on the starboard bitt knee and frantically smothering each handful as it slid reluctantly down. The top ten feet or so I left. 'Get a lashing round it,' I shouted to Mollie as I ran to the wheel. J & M had not broached—she had

Nᴇ

gone the other way and was on the point of a gybe. Frantically I gave her full port helm.

Kester came up through the after cabin. 'The bilge, Nobby,' he said excitedly: 'it's all run forward.'

'I know,' I snapped. 'Give Mollie a hand with the stays'l.'

J & M was still picking up speed, but with the almost over-whelming pressure of the staysail removed she slowly assumed a more natural stern-down position. Hastily I cranked on the wheel until I had settled her down on a reasonably straight course. Mollie was trying hard to pull down the peak of the staysail, and with Kester's help the job was soon done.

I looked round for Sym and Tigger, but presumably they had rushed below at my first panic-stricken shout. They were not on deck.

Mollie and Kester came back anxiously to the wheel. 'Should we get some of the mains'l off her?' Mollie asked.

'Or ruck the tops'l?' Kester suggested.

I looked round carefully. The seas were rising rapidly, and white horses were already beginning to break, but the wind (after the initial shock) was not too bad—certainly no higher than it had been at any other time on the passage. And it seemed to have settled down.

'Now we've got the stays'l off, we can leave her as she is for a bit,' I told them. 'The faster we go, the sooner we'll arrive.'

J & M had built up speed to about seven, or perhaps eight knots. At this rate—and after the sluggish crawl of this morning —it seemed only minutes before we passed Orfordness. There was only one snag: we could not alter course to starboard as we rounded the point unless we gybed—and I did not intend to gybe in Force 6 with all her sails set.

I kept her as close to the gybe as I could in safety and asked Kester to get me the next chart. As far as I could judge we were in a direct line to the Gunfleet—miles off course to port if I wanted to make Harwich Harbour. But if I wanted to get into Harwich I would have to gybe—or wear ship by winding. I nursed her along on the point of the gybe with the same care that I worked her to windward. Bloody wind!

The chart showed that we were not heading quite so badly off-course as I had supposed, but unless I intended to go all the way through the Wallet to the Colne or the Blackwater we would have to get the spreet over to port. We couldn't even fetch Walton Backwaters, let alone Harwich, on this gybe.

I explained the situation to Mollie and Kester.

'We'll have to half-brail the main, and ruck the tops'l, to gybe in this wind,' I told them. 'That means all the labour for nothing, because we'll have to set the lot again to get into harbour. I think the best thing we can do is try to get round by winding—but it's going to be a bit dicey in this blow.'

All these preliminaries had taken some time, and by now we were at least four miles offshore—roughly opposite to the red cliffs and radar installation of Bawdsey. I felt sure that the wind had increased: the white horses were no longer individuals, each was leaving its froth on the back of each wave, so that the spindrift extended in streaky lines as far as the eye could see; and some of it, now, was airborne—flung spume. This meant Force 7!

We took our time. We had plenty of space under our lee, and I told myself that if the worse came to the worst we could always bear away up the Wallet and shelter in the Colne. But that meant more hours at the helm and I was getting desperate. No! We'd damn' well get her into Harwich.

Mollie stood by the bowline to starboard, and Kester stayed aft. For the first time since the morning before, I closed the entrance hatch, trapping Sym below. As with the Holkham Bay tack, I shut the after hatch too. Kester had removed the starboard rolling wang and fastened it to the foot of the spreet; I had told him to do this because I was sure that we would not need them any more on this trip.

When the wind hit us, after backing four points, the sails had not received the full pressure of the initial squall because they had been trimmed for reaching—not for a run. I had seen no point in changing them. Now, I altered course to port, bringing the wind on our port beam and heading directly offshore. I watched the breaking seas closely, waiting for a 'smooth'—

but I couldn't find one in the chaotic seaway. Oh well, I thought, here goes. I gave her full helm to port.

She started to round up into wind at a spanking pace. I fidded the wheel, lowered the port leeboard, and cranked mightily to raise the starboard—trying all the while to ignore the furious smashing and thrashing cacophony of the flogging sails and gear. As I straightened up to rush back to the wheel, I noted that the foresail was still flogging—and Mollie being flung back and forth, still desperately hanging on to the bow-line—and that the mizzen was still drawing *on the port tack*.

Without thinking, I hurriedly refitted the capstan handle and lowered the starboard leeboard again. I was just in time. As *J & M* slowed to a stop, the pressure of wind on all her gear forced her astern; the rudder—fully over to port—caused her stern to move to port, and therefore the bows fell off to star-board on her original course. If I had not lowered the starboard leeboard promptly before pressure came on it, I would not have been able to get it down once we started sailing again.

With a succession of thuds and crashes, the sails filled, and we began another dash across the now-furious seas.

Mollie came aft. She looked desperate. 'I couldn't hold the sail against this wind,' she cried. 'I just couldn't hold it.'

'Don't worry.' I tried to soothe her. 'We've got plenty of sea-room. We'll try again in a minute.'

A bloody quick minute, too, I thought as I looked out to port and saw the blade of our one-ton leeboard surfing on its side some ten feet from the barge. It was an appalling sight— doubly so, because it was the weakest leeboard! The sickness of anxiety welled into my throat.

'Come on, darling,' I said encouragingly. 'Let's have another bash at it. This time, take three turns round the shroud and toss the end twice over the standing part, *and stand back*. You can't hold it in this wind.'

I watched her go reluctantly forward, and set up the bow-line. Now, I thought, this time—*please*!

I eased *J & M* a little closer into wind, until the topsail began to lift warningly, then I spun the wheel to port and fidded it.

Once again I rushed to starboard and cranked up the leeboard. Because I only had one chore instead of two, I was back at the wheel long before *J & M* really started to fight.

She spun readily enough into the wind. Then, as the foresail fell slack and began to flog violently, she hit a wave squarely, which foamed up across the bow rails and cascaded across the foredeck, forehatch—and poor Mollie. The wave stopped *J & M* as if she had bashed into a brick wall. The bows rose to the next breaker—on exactly the same point of the horizon. . . .

I was just about to make a dash for the starboard capstan once more when Mollie literally flung herself at the madly flogging foresail. I noticed then that one tiny area at the leech was bellying *inwards*—*J & M* had just passed the eye of the wind. The bowline-held sail tried to flick her off, but she forced her hands into the red canvas, adding just that tiny bit more windage to the sail. Slowly—very slowly—the bows paid off to port, gathering speed bit by bit as the foresail caught the wind. I helped, too, by centring the helm—just in case we were making a sternboard. We were round!

Now, on a reciprocal course, we were heading towards the red cliffs of Bawdsey which must have been about five miles away. *J & M* was griping viciously, boring up into wind at the slightest excuse, so that I had to give her almost full opposite helm to correct the swing. Within minutes on this new course I realised that we would have to get sail off her: she was on the verge of becoming uncontrollable.

It took nearly all my strength to move the wheel a spoke in either direction. I had to face it end-on, pull with both hands at the top spoke and at the same time push with one foot on a bottom spoke, in order to move it all. The pressures on the rudder—and on the not-so-good port leeboard!—must have been tremendous. It was quite impossible to bear away; it was as much as I could do to hold her on a reach.

I had no idea of our speed, although we were certainly exceeding eight knots. To leeward, an area of yeasty foam was all that remained of each wave which had been pulverised by *J & M*'s high bows, and we were making so much leeway that we were driven endlessly over the turmoil of our own progress. Our churned wake angled away from the starboard quarter— showing something like fifteen degrees of drift—until it was consumed in the general spindrift and flung spume of the angry seas.

Mollie and Kester waited anxiously for me to tell them what to do. I could not believe that we could win this battle, but our only hope was to try.

'You'll have to get some of the mains'l off her,' I told them. 'I'll keep her as much into wind as I can, to take a little pressure off the sail, and I'll let go the mainsheet bit by bit. It'll need you both on the brail winch handle. You know how to do it.'

'Could I take the wheel?' Mollie asked.

'Not a hope. I can barely hold her myself.'

They went forward along the weather deck—the lee rail was mostly submerged in bubbling surf—and edged down the sloping mast-deck to the winch. The invading sea swirled round their feet. They fitted the winch handle—Mollie back-to-rigging, Kester back-to-mast—and tried to crank. They did not even crank one pawl.

'Hang on!' I shouted.

I waited for a chance, fidded the wheel, waded into the scuppers, unhitched the mainsheet from the spiked block and released a few feet. Because there was so much wind, the sail remained as full as it was before.

'Now try,' I called.

This time they managed to crank a few pawls.

Then I released a little more mainsheet. . . .

Then they cranked a few more pawls. . . .

Every so often, Kester had to overhaul the middles and lowers to prevent them from snarling up, whilst Mollie leaned breathlessly against the winch. Kester did not have the weight to do more than this with the brails, but it was a help. As the main brails dragged the mainsail inch by inch towards the mast, and the pressure of the wind on the sail lessened, so *J & M* came more upright. Bit by tiny bit. . . .

It took forty long, long minutes. . . .

We were getting closer and closer to the dangerous shoals at the entrance to the Deben. . . .

'That'll do,' I shouted at last. It wasn't really enough—the main was still barely half-brailed—but we were running out of searoom. 'Kes, let go the tops'l halliard.'

I knew that neither Mollie nor Kester could overhaul the clewline after that struggle with the winch. I watched Kester closely as he lifted the coiled halliard off the cleat, capsized it on deck (clear of his feet!) and reached up to unfasten it.

'Hang on!'

I was ready with the fid.

I sprinted up the starboard deck, whipped the clewline off the cleat on the middle shroud. . . .

'Let go, Kes!'

I looked aloft. As the headstick moved, I flung all my weight on the clewline. Perhaps my pent-up anxieties, and my know-ledge that I had only seconds of time, gave me superhuman strength, or perhaps the hoops slid easily over the freshly-greased topmast; whatever the reason, I had the clewline taut, the topsail safely rucked, and was back at the helm before *J & M* had decided whether to luff or bear away.

It was just as well. The Bawdsey cliffs looked awfully close.

'Come aft,' I called to Mollie and Kester. 'Leave the ropes.'

J & M was steering a little easier now, although her speed seemed unaltered. I gave her port helm, then some more. . . . For a few seconds it seemed that she was determined to keep going until she dashed herself ashore amongst the welter of vicious surf which broke on the Deben Bar. Reluctantly the bows began to swing to port. Then we were round, and once again we were racing downwind—this time on the other gybe.

From beginning to end it had taken us about an hour to wear ship.

Mollie was absolutely exhausted. She sank wearily on the after coachroof.

'Will we be able to make it?' she asked. 'I can't stand much more.'

17. CLIMAX

I steered for the Cork lightship.

Now that we were running before the wind, and not battling against it, it no longer seemed quite so antagonistic. The hot sun quickly dried the decks, which minutes before had been knee-deep in swirling water. Kester propped open the main entrance, and Sym staggered wetly on deck. (Everything must be soaked down below, I thought suddenly.)

I had no doubt that many of the holidaymakers on the Felixstowe beaches would be watching our seemingly distressed condition. The part-brailed mainsail bulged six red, round caverns from peak to foot between each semi-confining brail, and the topsail bellied and flopped in the gusts and eddies like an expiring lung as *J & M* pitched and lurched and reeled along in a smother of foam like a clipper ship in the Roaring Forties. She must have looked quite a sight from a distance, but all the gear was holding up to the strain and we were in no immediate danger.

The topmast was O.K.; the topsail had not split any further; the port leeboard was still with us; the skiff still hung in the davits. . . .

The only real bother was the mess down below which we would have to clear up. But in this hot sun it would soon dry out. . . .

I reckoned we must be making at least twelve knots over the ground with the tide. . . .

And she no longer griped. She was steering easily now. . . .

The sun was so warm, so comforting. . . .

'You know,' I said dreamily to Mollie, 'I wouldn't half like a nice cup of tea.'

'All right, I'll go and make some.' Then, anxiously: 'Will there be time?'

I awoke to my responsibilities. It was so easy to drift away into a semi-somnolescent state—and so difficult to face-up to the brutal fact that somehow I had got to stop this mad charge downwind. I felt I could sit here for hours in the hot sunshine, just steering dreamily and watching the racing seas. . . . It was glorious! Come on, old girl, show 'em on shore what you can do.

Will there be time?

No! Of course there won't!

Reluctantly I dragged my mind back from its happy depths of silent contemplation to the present urgent realities.

The speed at which we were being driven downwind was awe-inspiring, frightening, and a little hypnotic. Even although we were under greatly reduced sail, which was still only trimmed for a reach, our speed must have been very nearly the maximum possible for her waterline length. And you cannot drive a sailing ship of *J & M*'s size through rough seas at maximum speed without creating quite a disturbance. We creamed through an incessant violent surf of our own making in a continuous thunder of churning water.

I tried to think. . . .

The thought of bringing this gale on to our starboard beam —which would have to be done if we turned into Harwich Harbour—was too frightening to consider. I told myself that it would only be a matter of minutes before we were behind Landguard Point and into sheltered water where we could anchor, but I just could not bring myself to turn and face the wind anymore. The wind had beaten me into submission at last; I had faced it fairly and squarely for three days and two nights—now I was finished. I couldn't take any more.

Walton Backwaters was the simple way out. The entrance lay more-or-less directly ahead of us, and we had been in there several times before, so I knew what it was like. We could anchor behind Stone Point (a misnamed place if ever there was one, because Stone Point was made up almost entirely of soft

sand), or up Hamford Water if the Walton Channel entrance was too difficult to attempt in this wind. The only problem was to locate the Pye End buoy amidst the confusion of spindrift and spray which seemed to be getting worse and worse as we charged along.

We drove past the Cork lightship like a demented runaway horse. The crew lined the deck. They all waved. I had the impression that they were cheering. . . .

Then we were on the last leg, heading towards an embayed lee shore with absolutely no hope whatsoever of spotting the hidden entrance to the landlocked haven unless we could see the buoys which marked the channel through the shallow Pye sands which covered the whole of Pennyhole Bay to port, and the Dovercourt shore to starboard.

Just in case, I took one last precaution. I lowered the starboard leeboard.

I sent Kester up forward with the binoculars. 'Any buoy,' I told him, 'just yell and point.'

We thundered across the entrance to Harwich Harbour. The Pitching Grounds were aptly named.

Somewhere dead ahead we should soon be seeing the Pye End buoy. Dovercourt began to close in to starboard. We were now inside the bay; there was little or no hope of escaping. . . .

The wind seemed to increase; the flung spume made a wet mist across the whole wave-tossed bay, which restricted visibility. Mollie, to port, searched desperately for the Pye End; Kester must have been doing the same. . . . Not a sign.

I altered course to port, knowing the danger of going too far to starboard and ending up on the Dovercourt Beaches. Between holding my barge right on the point of a gybe, and peering towards the flat sandy shore for some indication of where the entrance lay, I, too, was searching to port, to starboard—anywhere for the sight of a buoy. *Any* buoy!

The minutes passed. . . .

Now the shore ahead was so close that I could see a solitary man walking along the beach . . .

I knew then that we had lost the fight. I had made the fatal

mistake of allowing Nature to bully me into an unseamanlike
action. I had risked everything in a mad dash to leeward,
towards a lee shore, because I was too tired and too frightened
to turn against tempestuous forces any more. Now came the
automatic pay-off for such indiscretion. All that was left for me
to do was steer *J & M* straight up on the sandy beach dead
ahead; but the water was shallow, and the tide flowing: soon
she would refloat, the wind would swing her stern, the seas
would pound against her side. . . . Shipwreck!

The port leeboard touched the iron-hard sands, and the
pendant rattled on deck. We had less than two fathoms under
us! I was beginning to freeze in anticipation of what would
happen to us in a few seconds time. . . .

And then Kester yelled frantically.

'Nobby! Nobby! A buoy! To port!'

He was pointing urgently: off the port beam. I peered round
the bulging mainsail. There it was! No more than a hundred
yards away. It was a channel marker.

I gave her a little port helm—she didn't need much as we
were already sailing very nearly by the lee. For the first time
since I owned her, *J & M* seemed to question my decision: she
hung for a moment on the verge of the shore breakers and
refused to go.

'Go on, girl,' I breathed. 'Gybe. There's no alternative.
You've got to go.'

She lifted her stern to the next wave and started to bore
round to port. As she began to turn, so did I begin to meet her
on the helm—we couldn't afford to broach-to here. For one
appalling second she hung almost parallel along a trough
between breakers, and then she gybed and rolled at the same
moment. I had a momentary glimpse of the spreet—that
Sword of Damocles—whipping across the sky like a gigantic
windscreen wiper, followed by a teeth-rattling THUD! as it was
brought up all-standing by the wangs, then we were heeling to
starboard, over, over. . . . The roar of agitated bilge-water rose
above the din; I felt the additional jerk as it woo-o-o-shed
against the starboard side. Over, over—as much, if not more,

than she had heeled in the Humber. She dipped her rails. . . .
A wave smashed against her exposed bottom, sending an
explosion of wind-driven spray over us.

Then, viciously, she reverse-rolled—upright and over to
port, so that she gathered more water over her port rail. The
spreet swung across our heads . . .

'Quick,' I shouted to Mollie. 'Take in the slack: port wang!'

She let go of Sym and uncleated the fall, heaving in the rope
hand over hand.

'Watch out! Cleat it!' I had no time to say more. I was
desperately fighting the wheel as I watched the bows swinging.

The spreet hung to port aimlessly for perhaps two seconds,
and then crashed across again to starboard. Mollie had caught a
turn around the cleat, but at the precise moment of the next
roll to leeward her feet slipped on the spray-wettened deck and

she went down with a wallop. As we heeled she slithered to
leeward, beating the deck with her fists in sheer frustration. The
starboard wang met the strain of the spreet—just; the port
wang blocks screamed agony as the fall was ripped through
the sheaves.

Again *J & M* lurched sickeningly to port in a rapid reverse
roll. Mollie was still struggling to get up when Kester jumped
over her and hurled himself at the uncleated fall. In the few
seconds available he overhauled the festoons of slack, and as the
next roll to starboard commenced he caught a double turn on
the cleat and held it with professional exactitude. . . .

And we were in—it was as close as that.

Suddenly the seas were just choppy. I glanced briefly around.
We were just inside Hamford Water. I didn't bother about any
fancy anchor work.

I up-helmed as fast as I could wind the wheel, dropped the
fid, and ran forward. On the way I let go the foresail halliard.
J & M began to round up into the wind, but with very little
drive from the sails she was crabbing across the channel
towards Horsey Island. I humped the foresail folds from off the
windlass, whipped some slack chain across the barrel with my
right hand, whilst I prevented the anchor from dropping by
holding two turns pinned to the welts with my left, waited
until we reached the south side of the Channel, and then let the
anchor go with a run. I gave her fifteen fathoms. Then I
waited. She continued to crab sideways towards Horsey as she
took up the slack. There was an almighty crunch as the chain
bit into the welts on the windlass barrel; the chain rose bar-
taut from the water; *J & M*, at the end of the tether almost
flicked into wind; the mainsail and topsail began to flog; we
were safely anchored!

With Kester helping, I brailed the main, stowed the topsail
and lashed it to the shrouds, brailed the mizzen, and wound up
both leeboards—working leisurely in an ecstasy of blissful
relaxation after some sixty hours of continuous pressure.
Apart from thanking him for his prompt action which had
undoubtedly saved *J & M* from a dismasting (for the single

starboard wang would not have held a second time against the appalling force of the free-swinging spreet). I could not speak. Mollie had gone below, no doubt to contemplate the disasters in her department, and Sym, scenting the land, whined unhappily, forepaws on rail.

J & M was safe enough now. We were anchored just in Hamford Water, behind the mud bank (now covered by the rising tide), which marked the bend to port into Walton Channel, and behind Stone Point on the other side of this narrowest part of the channel. Stone—no, dammit, we always call it Sandy—Point lay dead to windward, giving us almost complete protection from the summer gale which still battered against the shores of Pennyhole and Dovercourt Bays. From aloft, as I lashed the topsail to the rigging, I looked down on those frightening, spindrift-covered seas and wondered how we had survived the last moments when disaster had actually struck. Kester spotting that buoy had been very nearly a miracle, because even from aloft I could only see the channel markers in our immediate vicinity—the rest were concealed in the maelstrom offshore.

Yet even in this short space of time, *J & M* once again looked as neat and tidy as though she had just been fitted-out for a summer's cruise, and hadn't yet put to sea. You can't go by appearances, I thought. The whole situation had rather a dreamlike quality: the backdrop of blue skies, burning sun, yellow sands, thundering breakers . . . the continuous wind . . . the absolute solitude. . . . We could just as easily be anchored inside a coral lagoon, with the trade winds thundering the surf on the reef outside. . . .

'Come on, Kes,' I called suddenly. 'Let's get the skiff in the water and take poor old Sym ashore.'

I called to Mollie, and answered her protests automatically: 'Half-an-hour won't make any difference, and a walk on dry land will do us all good.'

We unfastened the lashings, made fast the painter, and eased the skiff into the choppy water. Kester jumped down and unhooked the falls. Mollie did not have to urge Sym into the

boat—he hurled himself down in a scrabble of joy. We rammed
the thole pins into their holes—Kester at stroke, me in the bows;
Mollie hung on to Sym in the sternsheets. It was only a short
row.

We landed on the steep-to beach which miraculously is
never washed away; it was almost identical to the bank inside
Barton Haven. (My mind flicked back, I had a brief vision of
my first landing on that sunny bank, and then I returned to
this happier present.) Kester took the skiff's anchor up the slope,
dug a fluke into the soft sand and fastened the painter to the
ring. The skiff drifted a few feet offshore and meandered idly
in the puffs and eddies of breeze which the gale left behind in
this sheltered nook.

There were no yachts in the little bay up-channel behind
Sandy Point. We were quite, quite alone.

Sym went urinating-mad, beginning as soon as his paws
touched land. Kester ran and ran, around the Point and into the
full weight of the wind, pounding into it and then turning and
flying downwind until an extra puff sent him sprawling in the
soft, hot sand; again and again. . . . I joined him. It was marvellous. My pent-up repressions began to flow out of my body as
I lost control of both muscles and mind. It seemed that only a
frightful expenditure of physical energy could cleanse away
sixty hours—or was it sixty days?—of continuous strain. I
rejoiced in the wind—the hated, terrifying wind; now I loved
it; I thrashed into it, and revelled as it smashed and battered at
my straining body; I wafted with it, light and airy, down the
sand-slope, with scissoring legs unable to match the speed of my
descent. I crashed, hilariously, in a smother of sand, only to
scramble back again and again to repeat this mad dance of
happy salvation.

Until, finally, I flung my exhausted body down alongside
Mollie where she was sitting quietly at the top of the slope. . . .

And then came the reaction. . . .

The wind soughed through the coarse grasses on the lip of
the sand just over our heads. I lay on my back, breathing
deeply, looking up at Mollie, and the blue, blue sky, and the

waving grasses. And suddenly the void which I had just emptied needed filling, and a vast flood of emotion swept over me so that I actually choked with the assault. I wept like a frightened two-year-old, and the paroxysm of tears slowly cleansed my soul. It had never happened quite like this before, in spite of many other survivals from desperate ventures. I felt I had been reborn.

Only Mollie shared my experience, which was as it should be. Kester and Sym were furiously digging deep holes in the sand. To leeward, *J & M* strained at her anchor and looked every inch the queen she was. At that moment I loved her, as I loved Mollie and Kester and Sym and Tigger and life itself. It was good to be alive.

I fumbled in the pocket of my shorts and produced tobacco and matches.

18. DÉNOUEMENT

The transition from war to peace is not easy, as has been discovered by politicians over the centuries. We emerged from the battle, literally for our lives, and almost became lost in the limbo which followed.

The immediate problem of pumping-out *J & M* was solved so easily that I wondered what I had done wrong off Happisburgh. I topped-up the petrol tank of the sludge pump and it started first go; after just over two hours of continuous running it drained the bilges. Checking back over my every move, I learned that I had failed to unscrew the air vent on the filler cap. But this time I had done so automatically—although I was about thirty hours more tired. The lethargy of near-despair, caused by intense worry, is an insidious foe.

By eight o'clock the interior was as it had always been; the late afternoon and evening sun had remained hot enough, and the dying gale strong enough, to dry out every bit of seemingly sodden woodwork.

By nine, the wind had dropped to a gentle breeze. When the sun dipped behind the low Essex hills to the west, Hamford Water was glassy calm, and the evening was so quiet that we could clearly hear the plops of leaping fish. It was very difficult to believe in what had happened.

That night I slept dreamlessly and deeply. We awoke at the normal time to another perfect summer's morning—and to the next problem.

There were sixteen shillings in the kitty, and we had nowhere to go. All around us, people were waking up, gulping breakfast, catching trains, and generally going about the rut-like chores of a Monday morning. We knew about them, but they knew nothing about us. Nobody had seen us arrive; nobody was interested that we were here. I had a most queer feeling that we were lost in limbo and we were no longer a part of the living world.

We decided firstly that we must have at least a little working capital, and so Mollie wrote to her father asking for £10. To post this letter we would have to row all the way to Walton-on-the-Naze, for it certainly was not worth working the barge to windward out of Hamford Water and sailing her up Walton Channel, because the over-populated yacht moorings would prevent us from getting closer than about a mile from the landing by the yacht club.

'We can row up with the flood, and come back with the ebb,' I said. 'It's not all that far—less than three miles each way.'

And so, the first day in sheltered waters, we rowed the heavy skiff some five miles or more to post the letter and buy milk and bread.

On the evening of the first day we moved *J & M* a mile and a half up Hamford Water and anchored off the entrance to Kirby Creek, and on the morning of the second day we worked up between the narrow mudbanks to a pool behind Skipper's Island. We were now about as far from civilisation as anybody could get within sixty miles of London. We were probably the first barge to sail these forgotten islands for many years; perhaps we would be the last.

These were secret waters, which we had explored in part before, although Kester had been too young to remember much about them. Now he was anxious to see them all, for he had read Arthur Ransome's wonderful adventure story of these parts, *Secret Waters*, and he wanted to discover for himself how much of the book was true. He had plenty of time, for we remained in the pool for six days whilst I examined every possible berth for *J & M*.

We rowed to Landermere, and surveyed the silted remains of the old barge wharf. We would have loved dearly to bring our ship to this tiny and forgotten Essex village, where once the

huffler David Lay was responsible for the safe pilotage of all
barges through the network of channels which meander delta-
like from the westward end of Hamford Water. 'Once' was
fifty odd years ago, yet Landermere could not have changed
very much since pre-World War I—except that the wharf was
no longer usable. We wandered up and down the single street
which can only be reached by anybody via water because the
road which connects the village with civilisation is private,
across private property, and barred to the general public. We
saw nobody; the peace was absolute.

We rowed through the old, old man-dug 'cut' to Beaumont
Quay, at the western extremity of all these tortuous creeks.
This, too, was well-silted, although we could have berthed
there. It would have meant dropping the gear to get under
some low-slung power cables (Oh, how the scars of progress
infiltrate even the remotest places,) but what could we have
done once we poked *J & M* all the way up to this obscure
spot? I noted that Beaumont Quay was a possibility, and we
rowed back to Kirby.

We explored the Wade and Kirby Wharf, Oakley Creek
and Pewit Island, and even the 'cut' which leads to the old
explosives wharf. Kester, sculling alone in the skiff, explored
Horsey Island and Skipper's Island and many of the other
places mentioned in *Secret Waters*. He, at least, found much
evidence to show that Ransome had been here.

It was not an unhappy period, mainly, I suppose, because the
weather remained so exceptionally perfect. Early mornings and
late evenings were the best. All around us the world went about
its business, but nobody came near our pool and we remained
in complete isolation, broken only once when Mollie and
Kester walked the sea-walls and main road into Walton to
visit Post Restante, and then buy some necessary food.

But one must still make an effort—even in limbo. We were
getting nowhere from here; very well, we would move. On
the Monday, a week after our arrival, we set sail for Walton
Channel via Hamford Water.

Again we anchored—as near to the Town as we could get

in safety; again we explored. This time we rowed round
Hedge-end Island, then up Foundry Creek, and finally inspected
the saltings in the vicinity of the yacht club, including the creek
which wriggles up behind the boating lake and the houseboat
'pool' where a dozen or so barges in various stages of conversion
died slow deaths. But there was no satisfactory berth for *J & M*,
and certainly no berth of which we all approved.

'Have you been keeping a check on how far we've rowed
since we've been here,' I asked Kester on the last day.

'I make it forty-one miles,' he told me.

J & M was still the monster which controlled everything—
J & M, and lack of money. Somehow I had to find a berth for
her. Well, I had thought hard about it for nine days: during
the long rows, in solitary contemplation, and even in my sleep.
I had eliminated so many possibilities for good and sound
reasons that very little remained.

We had done our best to stay here, in peace. We had lived
well off the bounty of the sea: fresh cockles, lobsters, fish in
plenty. I had even toyed with the idea that it would not be
difficult to engineer a salt-water distillery and remain forever
independent of the land; that had been my original dream
before I bought my barge. But there was still Kester's schooling
—and Mollie. And I would have to make some money some-
time in order to pay for replacements to gear. I could see now
that the dream could only remain a dream: we had lived on the
fringes for a brief while, and now we had to go back to the
madness ashore from which we had been almost completely
isolated.

'There's Mistley,' I said. 'I think that's about our best chance.
Yachtsmen never go up the Stour, and Mistley has always been
a barging place. There're wharfs there, and a hard. Horlocks
used to build barges there, so they'll probably have blocks still
in use. There's not very much barging trade now, so I expect
there will be plenty of buckshee wharf space—and because
yachtsmen don't go there, we won't get stung. It's the most
likely place I can think of—and I've done a lot of thinking.
What do you say?'

Mollie said: 'Well, it's no good staying here any more. Do you think there's a school there?'

Kester said: 'Have you ever been there before, Nobby?'

I said: 'I went there when I was about your age, Kes, but I can only remember it vaguely. It used to be a lovely spot, and I don't suppose it's changed much in thirty years. There's bound to be a village school, and I'll bet it's a jolly nice one.'

And then: 'If we leave about eleven tomorrow, we can nip across to Harwich and take the early afternoon tide up the Stour. This evening we'll up-anchor and drift down to Sandy Point with the ebb—then we'll be in a good position to start in case the wind changes.'

In the absolute silence of a purple twilight we drifted down Walton Channel to the gentle urge of the ebb, with a light south-westerly breeze barely filling the staysail—the only sail I bothered to set. I dropped the anchor inside the tiny bay behind Sandy Point, and felt guilty for making such a racket. *J & M* swung to the tide, and nudged towards the restraining anchor as the heavy chain slackened. The current chuckled past the leeboards, and gurgled around the rudder as I set up the chain kicking strap and wound the wheel against it until it was bar-tight. Those were the only sounds in the stillness.

We made a last pilgrimage to give Sym a run ashore. I had to scull only a few yards to the steep-to beach on which we had landed so joyfully nine days before. Now we walked, almost sedately, around the point, and looked out towards the two clusters of pinprick lights which showed the positions of Dover-court and Harwich on the left, and Felixstowe on the right. In the centre, a purple gloom, broken occasionally by the brief wink from a buoy, indicated the route we would be taking on the morrow. The waves lapped gently on the sandy beach at our feet.

If only the sea could always be as peaceful. . . .

If only we could stop the world from changing. . . .

The weather could not have been kinder to us when we prepared to set sail next morning. The wind was light south-

south-west, and a few woolly trade wind clouds puffed across Pennyhole Bay like smoke from a cartoon train. As I unlashed the topsail, I looked towards the sea outside our haven, and saw how it sparkled and danced in the mid-morning sunshine—a invitation to set forth if ever there was one!

With wind and tide against her, *J & M* had her stern towards the entrance. We set the mainsail and mizzen, and I lowered both leeboards half-way, and cleated the wang falls, allowing some slack. Then all three of us went to the windlass to get the anchor—Mollie on one handle, Kester and I on the other.

The breeze was so light that the staysail barely filled as I hoisted it. But it helped *J & M* on her way a little. Later, the sun became decidedly hot, broken occasionally by the shadow of a cloud puff; it seemed to me that the wind was slowly fading. We hung in the entrance to Harwich until the tide turned.

Off the end of the long stone breakwater from the Harwich shore we gybed gently. The glassy waters were blue, and the sloping green fields and distant tree-lined banks of the Orwell looked like another country after the flatness of the Back-waters. Confused working sounds of Harwich came to us clearly across the calm water. We drifted very slowly upstream.

Presently a breath of moving air awoke our ideas. It was from the same direction as when we set out, and I was relieved. A little more westerly and we would have had to beat up the Stour! Within minutes the breath became a breeze, working through Force 1 and 2 until it steadied down to Force 3, possibly nearly 4. The flaccid sails filled, and *J & M* began to leave a bubbling wake behind her.

I steered across the Stour from Harwich, towards the con-glomeration of small boats and other grey-painted ships which were the floating part of the shore-based H.M.S. *Ganges*. I had previously decided to keep to the north shore of the Stour in order to avoid any possible complications as a result of meeting a Harwich/Hook-of-Holland passenger ship manœuvring out of, or into Parkstone Quay on the south bank. I had never sailed in these waters, and I wanted to keep clear of any possible dangers.

All the time the wind was very slowly increasing. There were certainly no threats from it as yet—Force 4 was a mere whisper after what we had been through.

We threaded through the *Ganges* moorings, passed Shotley Pier, and headed up the Stour with clear water ahead. I was relieved to find that the wind was just forward of our beam— we could make Mistley easily on one tack. It was still no more than Force 4, although now we were under the lee of Parkstone Quay—albeit quite a distance away—the tall buildings and ships alongside had disturbed the steady flow so that we were sailing in chunks and bumps of disturbance, with occasional brief periods of almost no wind at all. Our speed varied as the squalls came and died.

There was no warning at all of the last attack.

A chunk of squall materialised viciously in a sudden fluster of foam thirty yards off our port bow. It was no more than ten yards in diameter. It whirled briefly, sucked spray from the chuckling wavelets, passed across our foredeck. . . .

The staysail creaked with the sudden load. The thin topmast bowed—over, over. . . . and broke—THUD—in exactly the same place as its predecessor. . . .

The squall, short-lived, vanished. . . .

I watched, and almost in slow-motion the upper two-thirds of the topmast arched to starboard and stowed itself in the rigging. *Exactly* as before—except that there must have been a final backdraft from the expiring squall, because the staysail stowed most of itself on deck.

And we were still sailing slowly up the Stour, on course for Mistley. . . .

None of us spoke. There was nothing to say. Kester dragged the peak of the staysail in over the rail, and I handed the wheel to Mollie and lashed the pole of the topmast to the rigging to prevent it from slipping overboard.

'We can make Mistley under fores'l and mains'l,' I told her as I went back to the wheel.

'What a lousy rotten shame,' she said with feeling. 'All that work ruined; everything to do all over again.'

'But we've made it,' I told her gently. 'We're in! Supposing it had happened off Wells, or going through Hemsby Hole, or off Bawdsey. . . . If it had to go, it couldn't have been at a better time. We've been lucky. . . .'

Kester was not so generous. 'It's not fair,' he told the sea as he stamped back to his position in the bow. 'It's just not bloody fair.'

I did not have the heart to bawl him out for swearing.

We made Mistley from Shotley Gate in under two hours. As we approached the wooded cliffs which overhang the wharf-lined bank, I knew that this haven was welcoming us home. Crippled, we were coming into harbour for the last time. Over and over again, Robert Louis Stevenson's jingle rang through my head:

'Home is the sailor, home from the sea,
And the hunter home from the hill.'

If ever there was a homecoming, this was it—and yet I was a stranger to the place. Mistley: a clearing in a Mistletoe Forest. Mistley: developed as a shipbuilding and trading establishment by the Rigbys in the eighteenth century, and elaborately planned as a sea-bathing establishment by Robert Adam later in the century. Mistley: described early in the nineteenth century as 'the little dockyard, with ships building in the very bosom of a hanging wood'.

We came to Mistley, as we did to Landermere and Beaumont Quay, from the sea. There could never be an equivalent experience of going to those places by land. Perhaps this was some recompense for what we had suffered. The sea takes, but the sea also gives.

'Rest after toyle, port after stormy seas, death after life doth greatley please.'

A hundred swans cleared a path for us to nose alongside the wharf by the swan-spouting fountain which was the centre of this Georgian utopia.

And then the gods relented. . . .

In 'the large maltings office' which Rigby had built two
hundred and fifty years before, I met young Peter Horlock,
who managed the last of the fleet of Horlock's barges, and
occasionally skippered the all-steel *Portlight* which still traded
under sail. 'Help yourself to water,' he told me. 'Don't worry
about berthing charges.'

Later that afternoon he came aboard, and we told him everything about ourselves and our voyage. 'You can berth permanently alongside the old barge-building quay,' he said.
'We never use it now, and it's out of the way. It won't cost
you anything.'

Later still, we dollied downstream past the tall granary, the
coalyard, the boat slip, the hard, and the blocks, to the stone
quay which jutted out into the river. We nudged *J & M* into
this beautiful spot just in time before the tide left us.

A thousand swans escorted us, and then they drifted in
silence across the wide river towards a pink cottage which lay
on the far side under a shallow cliff, on top of which the gleam
of a vast cornfield was golden in the dying rays of the sun.
This, we remembered, was Constable country. This was what
England was all about. I had not known such peace for a long,
long time.

'Port after stormy seas . . . doth greatley please.'

Still later, when yellow lights were beginning to prick
through the velvet of the twilight, we had a visitor: a newly-
married wife who was searching for a converted barge which
she and her artist husband could live on.

That same evening, in the warm glow of the Aladdin-lit
saloon, I sold *J & M*, subject to survey, for £1,700.

Once again, manna from heaven. . . .

We swapped Mollie's sewing machine, which Peter's wife
wanted, for the discarded topmast from the Horlock's barge
Nellie Parker (which had been converted to power only). In
five days, with help once again from Kester, I shaved-down this
over-big spar to fit *J & M*'s topmast ironwork, removed the
two broken sections of the whippy Hull pole which had so
nobly survived the major part of the voyage, trundled its

sturdy replacement on board, repaired the 'H'-tear in the top-sail, and bent on and set up all the gear so that it was, once again, as good as new.

Whilst I worked, Mollie shopped, and Sym and Tigger were free to roam ashore as they liked on this entirely private and unseen patch of land—overlooked only by the driver of an occasional shunting engine which came down the steep slope from behind Mistley Station, backed into the tiny siding which was almost enveloped by trees and shrubs, and then switched the points to trundle over the bridge with the wrought-iron gateway which isolated our berth from the wooded cliffs.

I sent the sludge pump back to Owen Scrutton via the double burton on the spreet, into the skiff, upstream to the hand-wound crane on the wharf, on to a truck. In due course he acknowledged receipt, and said he was glad to hear that we had made it. I wrote, too, to Felton—but he never replied: perhaps the steel bars of responsibility now held him locked securely and forever.

And whilst we went about our respective chores, straighten-ing our affairs, we were visited regularly twice daily by the armada of graceful swans which are so much a part of Mistley.

J & M was surveyed ten days after our arrival by a grand-daddy of barge surveyors who remembered her being built, and he knew both Alf and Arthur White. After two whole days of looking into her innermost secrets, he passed her 'in excellent condition for her age'. He found it hard to believe that we had just sailed her, without additional crew, from the Humber.

The new owners gave us six weeks to move—which was generous. They paid up in full as soon as they received the survey report—which was more than generous.

And so the days continued to pass very pleasantly in our private haven before we had to move on again. Tigger grew fat and sleek from a diet of tasty rabbits and sundry game which he hunted through the paradise of untrodden woodlands (he even eyed the swans with malicious intent as he went about his catty business of building up a score!), and Sym leisurely pursued a similar quest although he failed to catch anything— just chasing or barking was more than enough for him in the absence of the more-usual gongoozlers.

Mollie shopped, and kept *J & M* as spick and span below as ever, and was happy with our temporary affluence. But she worried about the future: 'What are you going to do now?' she kept asking.

Kester—and I—were more than happy in this perfect haven of privacy. We explored everything—on both sides of the river. The days passed in a blur of utter contentment. I prolonged this pleasure for as long as possible, for it is as well to accept with gratitude these brief moments of happiness which the gods, or fate, deal out so grudgingly—and so seldom.

Idly, over the fleeting days, I had tried to find a suitable house, or another boat, for us to live in. £1,700 was not a lot of money. I still had no job. Kester would have to go back to school when the summer holidays were over. We had not resolved any problem by sailing south—except, fortuitiously, selling *J & M*.

So, reluctantly I returned to the civilised world and to commercialism. Peter Horlock had found a 45-foot twin-screw steel motor yacht at Henry Fox's yard at Ipswich at a price which I could afford. We went to see this—ugh!—motor boat. There was no doubt that the accommodation was excellent. £1,500 they were asking. Her name was *Waldemar*.

Time was running out on us: we had only a week left. We had to go.

I offered £1,250. Three days passed. The owner accepted. Peter put me on to a local lorry owner-driver and we agreed a figure for moving all our belongings from Mistley to Ipswich. On the day before the six weeks expired we left paradise, and *J & M*, forever.

I sat on top of our piled belongings, nursing Sym (who was not accustomed to road travel), as the lorry climbed, in whining bottom gear, the sandy track which traversed the cliff from the now-locked iron gates. Mollie was in front with Tigger, and

Kester leaned on the cab to enjoy the road ahead and relish the wind created by our progress.

But I looked back, as one always does when there have been happy memories—back, and down on my ship, where she lay alone, awaiting the next adventure. The last I saw of her was the fluttering new bob which Mollie had made (we kept the old one—a pathetic gesture on my part), and the scarlet tip of her canted spreet.

We stopped briefly at the top of the hill, whilst I left the key of the iron gates with the landlord of the pub for Peter to pick up. Then I climbed back on the lorry and joined Kester leaning on the cab. I did not look back again.

BIBLIOGRAPHY

by

Kester J. Clarke

BENHAM, HERVEY, *Down Tops'l: story of the East Coast sailing barges*, Harrap, 1951.
Last Stronghold of Sail, Harrap, 1948.

BENNETT, ARTHUR SCRIVENER, *June of Rochester, Topsail Barge*, Arnold, 1939; re-issued 1949.
Tide Time, Allen & Unwin, 1949.

CARR, FRANK GEORGE GRIFFITH, *Sailing Barges*, Hodder & Stoughton, 1931; revised edition, Peter Davies, 1951.

COOPER, FREDERICK STEPHEN, *A Handbook of Sailing Barges: Evolution and Details of Hull and Rigging*, Coles, 1955; second impression, 1967.
Racing Sailormen, P. Marshall, 1963.

DAVIS, DENNIS J., *The Thames Sailing Barge: Her Gear and Rigging*, David and Charles, 1970.

HERBERT, SIR ALAN PATRICK, *The 'Singing Swan'* (Fiction), Methuen, 1968.

IONIDES, CYRIL and ATKINS, JOHN BLACK. *A Floating Home*, Chatto & Windus, 1918.

LARKEN, PEGGY, *'Five Sisters'*, Hale, 1970.

MARCH, EDGAR JAMES, *Spritsail Barges of the Thames and Medway*, P. Marshall, 1948; reprinted, David and Charles, 1970.

MARTIN, EDWARD GEORGE, *Sailorman*, Oxford University Press, 1933.

PERKS, RICHARD HUGH, *A History of Faversham Sailing Barges*, Society for Spritsail Barge Research, 1967.

ROBERTS, A. W., *Coasting Bargemaster*, Arnold, 1949.
Last of the Sailormen, Routledge and Kegan Paul, 1960.